Literacy by Design™

Writing Resource Guide

Rigby®

A Harcourt Achieve Imprint

www.Rigby.com

1-800-531-5015

Contents

Using the Grammar Lessons and the Writer's Handbook . . iii
Using the Writing Organizers iv
Using the Writer's Craft Lessons v
Writing Assessment Rubric vi
Snapshots of Young Writers viii
Writing Assessment Rubric Form xi
Managing Writing Workshop xii

GRAMMAR LESSONS

Theme 1
Subjects and Predicates 1
Subject-Verb Agreement 2

Theme 2
Simple and Compound Sentences 3
Compound Subjects and Predicates 4

Theme 3
Review Sentence Structure 5
Declarative/Interrogative 6

Theme 4
Imperative/Exclamatory 7
Review Sentence Types 8

Theme 5
Making Compound Sentences 9
Sentence Combining 1 10

Theme 6
Sentence Combining 2 11
Review Sentence Combining 12

Theme 7
Common Nouns 13
Proper Nouns 14

Theme 8
Singular and Plural Nouns 15
Singular/Plural Possessive Nouns 16

Theme 9
Contractions 17
Pronouns and Antecedents 18

Theme 10
Singular and Plural Pronouns 19
Subject/Object Pronouns 20

Theme 11
Adjectives 21
Comparative and Superlative Adjectives 22

Theme 12
Articles 23
Review Adjectives 24

Theme 13
Action and Linking Verbs 25
Main and Helping Verbs 26

Theme 14
Present and Past Tense 27
Future Tense 28

Theme 15
Irregular Verbs 29
Review All Verbs 30

Theme 16
Adverbs 31
Review Adverbs 32

WRITING ORGANIZERS
Theme 1: Story Organizer 33
Theme 2: Sequence Organizer 34
Theme 3: Problem and Solution Organizer 35
Theme 4: Report Organizer 36
Theme 5: Poem Organizer 37
Theme 6: Main Idea and Details Organizer 38
Theme 7: Cause and Effect Organizer 39
Theme 8: Observation Log Organizer 40
Theme 9: Sequence Organizer 41
Theme 10: Procedural Organizer 42
Theme 11: Story Organizer 43
Theme 12: Compare and Contrast Organizer 44
Theme 13: Problem and Solution Organizer 45
Theme 14: Personal Narrative Organizer 46
Theme 15: Main Idea and Details Organizer 47
Theme 16: Letter Organizer 48

WRITER'S CRAFT LESSONS
Establish Setting 49
Build Strong Paragraphs 51
Include Figurative Language 53
Start Strong 55
End Effectively 57
Vary Point of View 59
Keep Language Fresh 61
Adapt to Purpose and Audience 63

Editing Checklist 65
Writer's Reflection Checklist 66
Writing Traits Checklist 67
Writer's Craft Checklist 68

Using the Grammar Lessons and the Writer's Handbook

Grammar is an essential element in effective writing. Without this fundamental knowledge, students cannot convey their message to an audience.

Lesson Background
- Provides an explanation of the grammar skill.

Teaching the Lesson
- Direct, explicit instruction on the conventions that need to be mastered.

- Refers to the Writer's Handbook for definitions, examples, and grammar rules.

Extending the Lesson
- Reinforces and applies the strategies and techniques targeted during Teaching the Lesson.

On Your Own
- Provides students with an opportunity to practice the skill on their own or with partners.

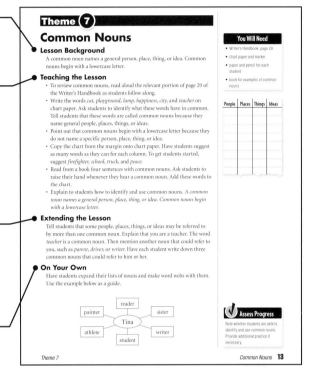

Using the Writer's Handbook
The Writer's Handbook is a valuable reference book for both teachers and students. It can be used with the grammar focus lessons in this guide or to introduce grade-level grammar skills. As students become familiar with grammar, they can use this book as a reference to answer questions about spelling, capitalization, grammar, and usage.

The Writer's Handbook is:

- For teachers to use as they teach focus lessons on grammar, usage, and mechanics during writing instruction.

- For students to use during the Writing Workshop.

Using the Writing Organizers

The Writing Organizers are reproducible graphic organizers that students use, first in groups and then individually, to develop concepts during prewriting. They are a basic framework for students' compositions. Before students use the Writing Organizers, they have participated in the shared writing process with a teacher using the Writing Transparencies. The Writing Organizer duplicates the graphic organizer used on the Writing Transparency.

Each Writing Workshop focuses on an organizational pattern or a writing form. When featured in explicit instruction, writing forms act as an important supportive frame in which students compose their own ideas. The Writing Organizers provide a hands-on, visual framework to help students organize their ideas and plan their writing.

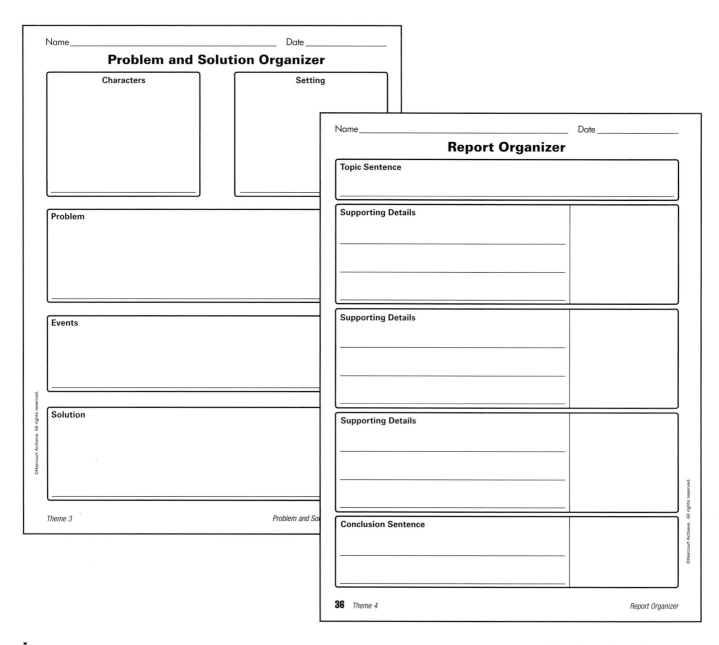

Using the Writer's Craft Lessons

Attention to writer's craft – which covers a host of tools and topics – is an essential way to improve students' writing while reinforcing the notion that the writing process is a craft.

Lesson Background
- Defines the Writer's Craft strategy.

Teaching the Lesson
- Focuses on selections (on the blackline master) that provide a model of the strategy to be addressed in the lesson.

- Guided instruction allows students to analyze and practice the targeted skill in a whole group setting.

Extending the Lesson
- Reinforces skills, strategies, and techniques in small groups or independent writing.

- Focuses on applying the craft skill to students' own work.

On Your Own
- Provides practice in the skill individually or with a partner.

- Encourages the use of the Writer's Notebook.

Whole Group Activity
- Provides a text and an activity for students to practice the craft skill.

- The blackline master can be copied or made into a transparency for instruction.

Start Strong

Engage Your Reader with a Lively Beginning

Lesson Background
It is important to begin a piece of writing with a lively opening. Writers can use one of several techniques to create a strong introduction. Some writers begin by describing a scene in detail, while others present the big picture about a topic. This lesson will focus on using the big picture as part of an effective beginning.

Teaching the Lesson
- Copy and distribute the Start Strong Master on page 56 of this guide. You may wish to make a transparency of this page for use during whole-class instruction.
- Read the selection "Pizza Is Perfect" aloud as students follow along.
- After reading, discuss the selection with students. *Do you think any part of the passage needs improvement?* (the first sentence) *After reading the first sentence, were you excited to read the rest of the passage?* (no) *What is the big picture of this passage?* (People like pizza.)
- Tell students that a lively beginning helps engage readers from the start. One way to hook the reader in the opening is to give the big picture about a topic. Work with students to brainstorm possible ways to change the opening of "Pizza Is Perfect" in order to give the reader the big picture. You may ask *What information should be included in the opener? What would be a good way to make the opener interesting?*
- Have students revise "Pizza Is Perfect" to include an opener that presents the big picture of the passage. They may record a class suggestion or write a beginning of their own.

Extending the Lesson
During small-group writing instruction, have students select from their writing folder a recent piece of writing that they feel needs a more engaging beginning. Support students as they revise their writing. Then compare the original and revised versions as a group.

On Your Own
Have students look through other fiction and nonfiction texts in search of openers that engage the reader by presenting the big picture. Encourage students to record some of these examples in their Writer's Notebook as a source for strong beginnings.

✓ **Assess Progress**
Note whether students are able to craft engaging beginnings. Provide additional practice if necessary.

Writer's Craft   *Start Strong* **55**

Pizza Is Perfect

I like pizza. It is hard to turn down the tasty blend of cheese, sauce, and chewy crust. Another great thing about having pizza is the large list of toppings you can choose from. You can add everything from vegetables to meat. Some people even add fruit to their pizza. You can order pizza from a restaurant, but it is also easy to make at home. It is not hard to see why many people like to eat pizza.

Write a New Opening
Write a new opening sentence for "Pizza Is Perfect" by giving the big picture about the topic.

_____

_____

_____

_____

_____

56 *Writer's Craft*   *Start Strong Master*

Writing Assessment Rubric

The *Literacy by Design* Writing Assessment Rubric contains key behavioral indicators for holistically evaluating the development of young writers. Use the rubric not only to identify the developmental stage of your students but also to plot their future growth, both within and across stages. (See the Writing Assessment Rubric Form on page xi.)

	Experimenting Stage	Emerging Stage
Content Ideas and Organization	• Scribbles emulate the look of writing; some may carry meaning. • Simple illustrations represent ideas. • Student shares ideas orally; ideas may lack focus and may vary upon subsequent retellings. • Student may attempt organization by grouping scribbles or illustrations together.	• Illustrations begin to have more detail. • Student orally explains ideas and may elaborate on illustrations or written words and phrases. • Some ideas begin to take shape, but a clear message or storyline may not be present. • Organization continues to develop as student groups similar words and illustrations. • With prompting, student can state audience and purpose.
Language Sentence Fluency, Word Choice, and Voice	• Student shows an awareness that illustrations and written words are different. • Student knows letters and begins to experiment with sound-letter relationships, although some letters may be random. • Illustrations represent common words and generally lack distinguishing features.	• Student demonstrates understanding of one-to-one correspondence between written and spoken words (e.g., student points while reading). • Writing takes the form of simple, common words, phrases, or sentences. • Voice begins to emerge as student adds personal touches to writing and illustrations.
Mechanics Writing Conventions	• Student begins to show an awareness of left-right writing directionality. • Student writes strings of letters and may begin to group letters into words, whether pretend or actual. • Writing is not always legible.	• Clear words emerge, with proper spacing. • Student experiments with uppercase and lowercase letters. • Student begins to group words together into phrases and sentences, arranging them from left to right. • A number of words may be spelled phonetically.
Process Writing Purpose, Process, and Presentation	• Student relies on teacher prompting to draw or "write" about a specific idea. • Student talks about (or explains) work and can be prompted to add to it (e.g., can add more details to a drawing). • Final work may be scattered and disordered on page; illustrations may be labeled.	• Student understands the purpose of and relies upon a small number of text forms (e.g., story, letter). • With guidance, student talks to generate ideas for writing. • Student draws pictures or writes words/phrases about a specific idea. • Student can be prompted to add to the work and make simple corrections. • Final work is mostly legible and more organized; clear use of simple fiction and nonfiction text features (e.g., labels, titles) emerges.

Developing Stage	Proficient Stage	Advanced Stage
• Illustrations, if present, begin to support writing rather than substitute for writing. • A message or storyline is present but may lack a clear beginning or a clear ending. • Some ideas are supported with details but may lack focus. • Ideas show a more formal attempt at organization; some sequencing and use of simple transitions (e.g., words such as *next* or *then*) may be present.	• A clear message or storyline is present, with a serviceable beginning and ending. • Ideas are focused and supported with sufficient details; some details may be weak or off topic. • Ideas are generally well organized; student begins to use more complex transitions to achieve greater passage-level coherence (e.g., transitions that link key content and ideas from sentence to sentence). • Student begins to make choices about ideas and organization to suit audience and purpose.	• A clear message or storyline is present, with an engaging beginning and ending. • Ideas are focused and fully supported with strong, relevant details. • Ideas are well organized; use of transitions and other devices results in writing that is smooth, coherent, and easy to follow. • Student makes strong, effective choices about ideas and organization to suit audience and purpose.
• Simple and compound sentences are used in writing. • Student begins to experiment with different sentence types and syntactical patterns that aid fluency, but overall writing may still be choppy. • Student correctly uses and relies upon a small bank of mostly common words; student may begin to experiment with less common words. • More frequent hints of voice and personality are present, but writing continues to be mostly mechanical.	• More fluent writing emerges through the use of an increasing variety of sentence types and syntactical patterns. • Student correctly uses a large bank of common words; student effectively experiments with new words and begins to choose words more purposefully (e.g., to create images or to have an emotional impact). • Voice continues to develop as student experiments with language.	• All sentence types are present. • Student writes fluently, varying sentence types, sentence beginnings, and grammatical structures. • Student uses an extensive bank of common and less common words correctly; student successfully uses words with precision and purpose. • Voice is expressive, engaging, and appropriate to audience and purpose.
• Sentences have beginning capitalization and ending punctuation; student experiments with other marks (e.g., commas). • Paragraphing begins to emerge. • Spelling is more conventional, especially for high frequency words. • Awareness of usage (i.e., that there are rules to be followed) begins to develop; student experiments with simple usage conventions, but success is variable.	• Student correctly uses all marks of end punctuation; correct use of some other marks is evident, especially in typical situations (e.g., a comma before the conjunction in a compound sentence or a colon to introduce a list). • Student correctly spells most high frequency words and begins to transfer spelling "rules" to lesser-known words. • Writing demonstrates basic understanding of standard grade-level grammar and usage.	• Student correctly and effectively uses standard grade-level punctuation, including more sophisticated marks and usages (e.g., dashes to emphasize key ideas). • Student correctly spells a wide variety of words, both common and uncommon. • Writing demonstrates full and effective control of standard grade-level grammar and usage; overall usage aids reading.
• Student experiments with a variety of text forms and begins to understand how purpose determines form. • Student generates limited prewriting ideas. • With teacher support, draft shows some development but continues to be mostly skeletal. • Student revisits the work but mostly to correct a few line-level errors (e.g., end punctuation and spelling). • Student begins to move more naturally and independently through the writing process. • Final work is generally neat; an increasing variety of fiction and nonfiction text features (e.g., titles, headings, charts, captions) is present, but features may be more for show than for support of message.	• Student demonstrates increasing control over a variety of text forms and can choose form to suit purpose. • Student generates sufficient prewriting ideas. • Draft shows good development of prewriting, including effective attempts at focusing, organizing, and elaborating ideas. • Student revisits the work not only to correct errors but also to address some passage-level issues (e.g., clarity of message, sufficiency of details); student may use supporting resources (e.g., dictionary, grammar book). • Sense that the process is purposeful begins to emerge. • Final work is neat; use of various fiction and nonfiction text features tends to support and clarify meaning.	• Student effectively controls a variety of text forms and can choose form to suit purpose. • Student uses prewriting ideas as a plan that is both general and flexible. • Draft shows strong development of prewriting and may effectively depart from prewriting as a signal of the student's overall writing maturity. • Student revisits the work not only to correct errors but also to address key passage-level issues. • Overall, student shows investment in the craft of writing and moves through the stages smoothly and recursively. • Final work is neat; effective use of fiction and nonfiction text features results in a polish that strengthens the student's overall message.

Snapshots of Young Writers

Writing samples, or anchor papers, provide powerful snapshots of writing development—snapshots key to understanding students' control over written language and to determining subsequent paths of instruction. The following writing samples represent each of the five stages of development in the *Literacy by Design* Writing Assessment Rubric. The samples for each stage are preceded by a brief summary of key behavioral indicators for that stage.

Experimenting Stage

- Writing is mostly an attempt to emulate adult writing.
- It includes single letters, letter strings, and simple illustrations.
- Writing attempts to be communicative, but most letters and letter strings do not carry consistent meaning.

Nour

Mireya

Emerging Stage

- Writing shows an understanding that spoken words can be written down and read by others.
- It includes the use of content-bearing words, phrases, and short sentences.
- Writing may demonstrate left-right directionality and experimentation with capital letters and end marks.
- It includes many words spelled phonetically.

Ricky

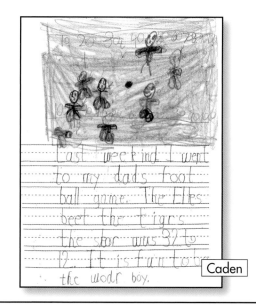

Caden

Developing Stage

- Writing exhibits growing control over writing conventions, including more conventional spelling, punctuation, and grammar.
- Writing carries a simple message supported by some details.
- Sentence structure is mostly formulaic and mechanical.
- It includes a limited number of text forms.

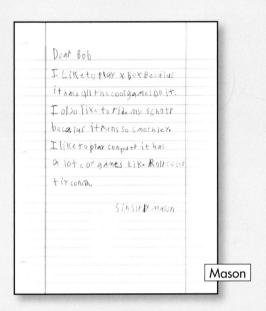

Mason

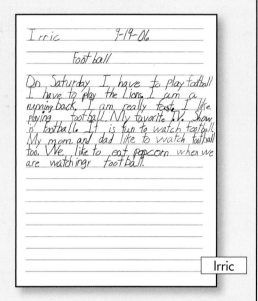

Irric

Proficient Stage

- Writing includes a clear, focused message supported by sufficient details.
- It exhibits most grade-level conventions.
- Writing includes a variety of sentence structures.
- It shows a growing awareness of audience and purpose.
- It demonstrates control over a variety of text forms.

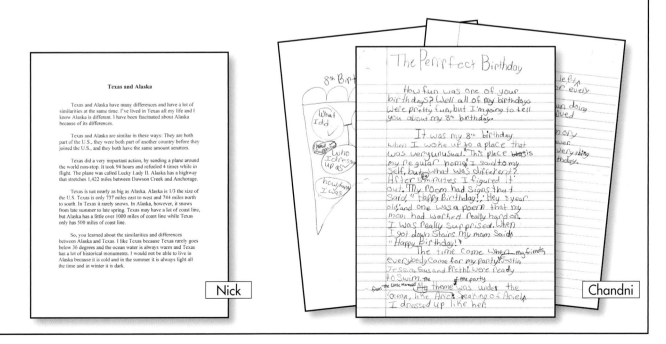

Nick

Chandni

Advanced Stage

- Writing demonstrates mastery of conventions and purposeful variety of sentence structures.
- It includes a strong, focused message that is fully supported and engaging in presentation.
- Writing exhibits a clear understanding of audience and purpose.
- It shows effective use of word choice, voice, details, and text form.

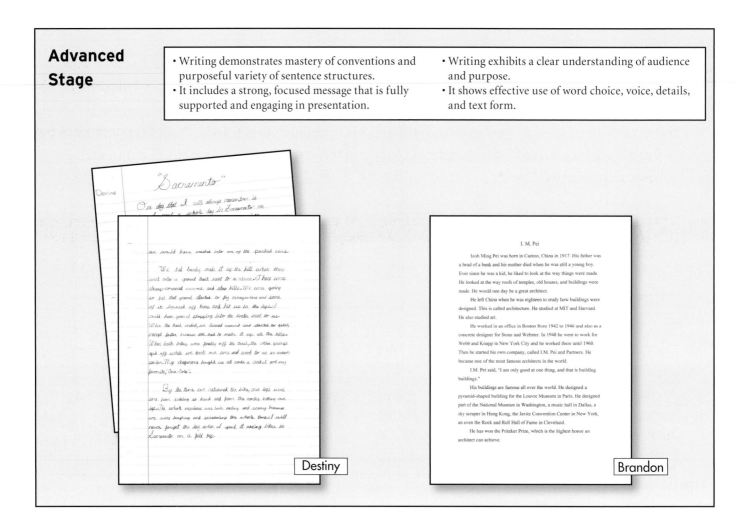

Destiny

Brandon

Writing Stages According to Grade Level

	Experimenting Stage	Emerging Stage	Developing Stage	Proficient Stage	Advanced Stage
Grade K	▨				
Grade 1		▨			
Grade 2		▨			
Grade 3			▨		
Grade 4				▨	
Grade 5				▨	

Writing Assessment Rubric Form

Student's Name _____   **Date** _____

① • Based on an initial review of a representative sampling of student work, identify the student's most likely stage of development. Locate that stage on the rubric and then review the behavioral indicators for each of the four instructional categories: Content, Language, Mechanics, and Process.
• If the indicators for a particular category mostly describe the student's work, check the appropriate box.
• The student is considered to be in a particular stage if at least three category boxes in that stage have been checked. If fewer than three boxes are checked, the student is considered to be in the previous stage.

	Experimenting	Emerging	Developing	Proficient	Advanced
Content Ideas and Organization	☐	☐	☐	☐	☐
Language Sentence Fluency, Word Choice, and Voice	☐	☐	☐	☐	☐
Mechanics Writing Conventions	☐	☐	☐	☐	☐
Process Writing Purpose, Process, and Presentation	☐	☐	☐	☐	☐

Stage _____

② • Note observations about key strengths and weaknesses.
• Tie observations to specific strategies to be used in future instruction.

Observations	Notes for Future Instruction
Strengths	➡
Growth Areas	➡

* It is recommended that you use the *Literacy by Design* Writing Assessment Rubric to evaluate a sampling of each student's writing at least three times a year.

Managing Writing Workshop

Independent Writing at the Core

Similar to reading workshop, writing workshop is the time when a teacher works with a small group of students to differentiate writing instruction. Other students are engaged in writing independently, whether that means generating ideas, writing a draft, or revising their writing.

Students learn to write with practice. They need ample classroom time to explore ideas and refine their writing skills. Independent writing allows students to apply the strategies and skills they are learning in whole class and small group instruction.

A key difference between small group writing and small group reading is that student writers are typically working on the same piece as they move from the group to independent work. In fact, a writer might continue work on the same writing piece over several small group sessions, continuing to work on the piece between sessions in independent writing as well. Having the two activities occur simultaneously in the same workshop emphasizes the connection between small group and independent writing.

Making Independent Writing Successful

- **Conference regularly with writers**. Meet with students to ensure they use their Writer's Notebook or other resources when recording ideas and finding writing topics (See *Comprehensive Teacher's Guide*, Writing Conference Form, page A23).

- **Provide a focus for independent writing**. Choose a writing form, organizational pattern, process, or trait that is taught in the theme to serve as a focus for students during independent writing.

- **Offer prompts when writers get stuck**. The best source for writing ideas is a student's Writer's Notebook, but occasionally students just get stuck. Provide specific prompts related to the theme's instructional focus that can be used when students are having difficulty identifying a topic for their writing.

Setting Up Writing Workshop

In a successful writing workshop, students understand and embrace the opportunity to explore ideas and mold those ideas into text. Planning requires setting up materials and creating an environment in which students can manage their independent writing time effectively.

Create a Space for a Successful Writing Workshop

- Designated place for students to keep their **writing folders** and **Writer's Notebooks**

- **Reference area** with dictionaries, encyclopedias, and thesauruses

- **Writing center** with magazines and other visual materials to spark ideas

- Wall space to display **shared** and **interactive writing pieces**

- Copies of **graphic organizers** to capture and organize writing ideas (see pages 33–48)

Subjects and Predicates

Lesson Background

Every sentence has a subject and a predicate. The subject includes the noun that performs an action and any words that describe the noun. The predicate contains the verb and any words that describe the verb. The predicate tells something about the subject.

Teaching the Lesson

- To review subjects and predicates, read aloud the relevant portion of page 34 of the Writer's Handbook as students follow along.
- Write the following on chart paper: *The older boy played basketball.* Ask students *Who played basketball?* Circle the words *The older boy.* Explain to students that *The older boy* is the complete subject of the sentence because it tells who performs the action.
- Ask students *What noun tells who played basketball?* Underline the word *boy.* Explain that *boy* is the simple subject.
- Next ask students *What did the boy do?* Underline *played basketball.* Explain that this phrase is the complete predicate. A predicate tells what the subject of the sentence does or did. It usually begins with the verb and includes all the words that describe the verb. Ask students *What is the action word, or verb, in this sentence?* (played) Explain that the verb *played* is the simple predicate.
- Now change *The older boy* to *Benjamin.* Ask students *Did the subject or the predicate change?* (the subject) Next replace *played basketball* with *joined the band.* Ask *Did the subject or the predicate change?* (the predicate)
- Explain the difference between a subject and a predicate. *In a sentence, the subject is the noun that performs the action and any words that describe that noun. The predicate is the verb and any words that describe the verb.*

Extending the Lesson

Draw the two columns in the margin on chart paper. Tape the sentence strips next to the chart. Have students tell you where to cut each sentence so that the subject and predicate are separate. Then ask a volunteer to tape each half in the correct column on the chart.

On Your Own

Have each student choose a book from the classroom and copy three sentences onto his or her paper. Ask students to underline the subjects in red and the predicates in blue. Have students exchange papers and check one another's work.

You Will Need

- Writer's Handbook, page 34
- books for subject and predicate examples
- chart paper and marker
- scissors and tape
- sentence strips with the following sentences written on them:
  The new teacher kept the class quiet.
  She loves mystery books.
  The young doctor saved the man's life.
  The old dog sat next to the little boy.
  My big, fluffy, yellow cat meows.
- paper, pencil, and red and blue colored pencils for each student

Subjects	Predicates

Assess Progress

Note whether students can identify subjects and predicates. Provide additional practice if necessary.

Subject-Verb Agreement

Lesson Background

A verb shows action or connects the subject to another word. Verbs can be singular or plural, but they must agree with the subject of a sentence. A singular subject must be paired with a singular verb, and a plural subject must be paired with a plural verb.

Teaching the Lesson

- To review subject-verb agreement, read aloud the relevant portion of page 24 of the Writer's Handbook as students follow along.
- Write the following sentence on chart paper: *Jin likes ice cream.* Explain that the subject, *Jin,* is singular; Jin is one person, so the sentence takes the singular verb *likes.*
- Write the following sentence on chart paper: *Jin and Anika like ice cream.* Explain that the subject, *Jin and Anika,* is plural because there are two people. That means that the verb, *like,* must also be plural.
- Draw a T-chart on chart paper. Label one column *Singular* and one column *Plural.* Tape the noun index cards next to the chart in random order. Tape the verb index cards next to the opposite side.
- Have students tape the noun index cards in the correct columns. When students finish, have volunteers choose a noun from the chart and a verb from the verb index cards and write a sentence using them.
- Explain how students can make sure the subject and verb in a sentence agree. *Remember that* singular *means one. Use a singular verb with a singular subject. Remember that* plural *means more than one. Use a plural verb with a plural subject.*

Extending the Lesson

Copy the sentences in the margin onto chart paper. Have students fill in the blanks with the correct form of the verb.

On Your Own

Give each student a book that you have in the classroom. Ask students to copy three sentences from the book onto a piece of paper. Have students identify whether the sentences have a singular or plural subject.

You Will Need

- Writer's Handbook, page 24
- index cards with the following verbs written on them: *smiles, draws, wash, swim, finishes,* and the following nouns: *Ana, Jaime, The brothers, The cat, Sharon and Mikael*
- books for sentence examples
- tape
- chart paper and marker
- paper and pencil for each student

---

1. Rosa ____ baseball with her cousin's team. (play/plays)

2. They ____ to Lincoln Elementary School. (goes/go)

3. Paul ____ his younger brother to school. (take/takes)

4. The dog and cat ____ their dinner in the kitchen. (eats/eat)

Assess Progress

Note whether students understand subject-verb agreement. Provide additional practice if necessary.

Simple and Compound Sentences

Lesson Background

Sentences can be simple or compound. A simple sentence expresses one complete thought. A compound sentence is made up of two or more simple sentences that are linked by a comma and a conjunction, such as *and, but,* or *so.*

Teaching the Lesson

- To review simple and compound sentences, read aloud the relevant portion of page 35 of the Writer's Handbook as students follow along.
- On chart paper, write *The teacher greeted my parents.* Say *This is a simple sentence because it expresses one complete thought. It has a subject and a predicate.*
- On chart paper, write *The teacher greeted my parents, but he didn't know their names.* Circle *The teacher greeted my parents* and *he didn't know their names.* Point out to students that each of the circled groups of words is a simple sentence. The two simple sentences together form a compound sentence. Ask students what word connects the two simple sentences. Draw a box around the comma and the conjunction *but.*
- Explain simple and compound sentences. *A simple sentence expresses one complete thought. A compound sentence is two simple sentences joined by a comma and a connecting word, such as* and, but, *or* so.

Extending the Lesson

Write the paragraph in the margin on chart paper. Have students circle the simple sentences and underline the compound sentences.

On Your Own

Give each student a fiction or nonfiction book from the classroom. Have them copy two simple sentences and two compound sentences on notebook paper. Then have partners exchange papers and label the sentences simple or compound.

LaToya hid quietly in the kitchen. She was waiting for her mother to come home. LaToya's mother opened the door suddenly, and everyone yelled "Surprise!" Her mother was scared at first, but then she saw her birthday cake and smiled.

Assess Progress

Note whether students can identify simple and compound sentences. Provide additional practice if necessary.

Compound Subjects and Predicates

You Will Need

- Writer's Handbook, page 34
- chart paper and marker
- books for examples of compound subjects and predicates
- paper and pencil for each student

Lesson Background

Sentences are made up of subjects and predicates, both of which can be either simple or compound. A simple subject is the noun that performs the action in a sentence. A compound subject is made up of two or more simple subjects. Similarly, a simple predicate has one verb, while a compound predicate is made up of two or more simple predicates.

Teaching the Lesson

- To introduce compound subjects and predicates, read aloud the relevant portion of page 34 of the Writer's Handbook as students follow along.
- On chart paper, write *The boy and his sister picked apples.* Have students identify both simple subjects. Circle *boy* and *sister.* Explain that the connecting word *and* connects the two subjects, making a compound subject.
- Write the following sentence on chart paper: *The puppies barked and chased a ball.* Have students identify both simple predicates. Underline *barked* and *chased.* Tell students that *and* is used here to connect the two verbs, making a compound predicate.
- Write the following sentences on chart paper: *Emily and Jency ran to catch the baseball. Carlos smiled and thanked the woman.* Have students underline the compound subject in the first sentence (*Emily and Jency*) and circle the compound predicate in the second sentence. (*smiled and thanked the woman*)
- Define compound subjects and predicates for students. *A compound subject is made up of two or more simple subjects. A compound predicate is made up of two or more simple predicates.*

Extending the Lesson

Copy the sentences and the table in the margin onto chart paper. Have students expand each of the three sentences on their own paper by adding one of the simple subjects and/or predicates from the boxes in the table. Have students circle the subjects and underline the predicates. Then tell them to label the compound subjects as *CS* and the compound predicates as *CP.*

On Your Own

Have each student choose a book and copy three sentences containing a compound subject or a compound predicate. Have students circle the subjects and underline the predicates. Then instruct them to label the compound subjects as *CS* and the compound predicates as *CP.*

Sentences

1. The science teacher gave a test.

2. The first grader walked to school.

3. The old dog learned a new trick.

Subjects	Predicates
the reading teacher	assigned homework
her friend	played on the playground.
the puppy	won a prize

✓ Assess Progress

Note whether students can identify sentences with compound subjects and predicates. Provide additional practice if necessary.

Review Sentence Structure

Lesson Background

A sentence is made up of a subject and a predicate. A simple sentence expresses one complete thought. A compound sentence is made up of two or more simple sentences that are linked by a comma and a conjunction, such as *and, but,* or *so.* A compound subject is made of two or more simple subjects, and a compound predicate has two or more simple predicates.

Teaching the Lesson

- To review sentence structure, read aloud the relevant portions of pages 34–35 of the Writer's Handbook as students follow along.
- Write the following sentence on chart paper: *Many students eat snacks after school.* Have volunteers circle the subject and underline the predicate.
- Ask students *Who else might eat snacks after school?* Have a volunteer make the subject compound. Point out that the sentence now has a compound subject. Next have students make the predicate compound by naming something else many students do after school. Point out that the sentence now has a compound predicate.
- On a new sheet of chart paper, write *We went skating. Later we threw snowballs.* Explain that these are simple sentences. Have a volunteer connect the sentences. Remind students that two simple sentences joined with a comma and a conjunction make a compound sentence.
- Review sentence structure. *A sentence has a subject and a predicate. The subject and predicate of a sentence can be simple or compound. A simple sentence expresses one complete thought. A compound sentence is made of two or more simple sentences that are linked by a comma and a conjunction, such as* and, but, *or* so.

Extending the Lesson

Tape the sentence strips to the board. Ask students to identify the compound sentence and the sentence with a compound subject and a compound predicate. Discuss the differences between the two types of sentences.

On Your Own

Copy the sentences from the margin onto chart paper. Have students copy the sentences onto their own paper and underline the subject(s) and circle the predicate(s) in each sentence. Then have them decide which sentences are simple sentences. Tell students to write the word *simple* next to those sentences. Students should then decide which sentences are compound and write the word *compound* next to those sentences.

1. The two sisters went on vacation and had a great time.
2. His uncle took him fishing, but they didn't catch anything.
3. The girl went swimming, so she was late for dinner.
4. The teacher and her students raised money and used it to buy new books.

Assess Progress

Note whether students understand sentence structure. Provide additional practice if necessary.

Declarative/Interrogative

Lesson Background

Sentences can have different purposes. Two kinds of sentences are declarative and interrogative. A declarative sentence makes a statement and ends with a period. An interrogative sentence asks a question and ends with a question mark.

Teaching the Lesson

- To review declarative and interrogative sentences, read aloud the relevant portion of page 35 of the Writer's Handbook as students follow along.
- Draw a T-chart on chart paper. Label the columns *Question* and *Statement*. Explain that a question asks something and ends with a question mark. In the *Question* column, write *Who are you?* Explain that a statement tells a fact or an idea. It ends with a period. In the *Statement* column, write *I am a teacher.*
- Ask students to imagine they are meeting George Washington. What questions would they ask? Write these in the *Question* column. How do you think George Washington would answer these questions? Write the answers in the *Statement* column. For each question and statement, point out the correct end punctuation.
- Read a passage from a book that has questions and statements in it. Ask students to identify sentences from the passage as either statements or questions and to name the correct end punctuation for each.
- Explain the difference between a statement and a question. *A statement tells a fact or an idea and ends with a period. A question asks something and ends with a question mark.*

Extending the Lesson

Write the paragraph in the margin on chart paper. Have volunteers add correct end punctuation. Then have students identify each sentence as a statement or a question.

On Your Own

Divide students into pairs. Have each student write a list of four questions about art. Then tell students to exchange papers with their partner and answer the questions with statements.

You Will Need

- Writer's Handbook, page 35
- chart paper and marker
- book excerpt that includes questions and statements
- paper and pencil for each student

Angelica thought about her new school ____

What would it be like ____

How much homework would she have ____

She hoped it would be as good as her old school ____

Would she be able to make friends at the new school ____

Assess Progress

Note whether students can identify and punctuate declarative and interrogative sentences. Provide additional practice if necessary.

Imperative/Exclamatory

Lesson Background

Different types of sentences have different purposes. An imperative sentence gives a command and generally ends with a period. An exclamatory sentence shows strong emotion or surprise and ends with an exclamation point.

Teaching the Lesson

- To review imperative and exclamatory sentences, read aloud the relevant portion of page 36 of the Writer's Handbook as students follow along.
- Write the following sentences on chart paper: *Get out your notebooks. We're going to the museum!* Circle the punctuation at the end of each sentence. Then explain that the first sentence is a command; it tells someone what to do. Commands usually end with a period. They sometimes end in a exclamation point, depending on how forceful the command is. The second sentence is exclamatory; it shows excitement. Exclamatory sentences end with an exclamation point.
- Write the sentences from the margin on chart paper, leaving off end punctuation. Read the sentences aloud with appropriate emphasis. Have volunteers identify each sentence as a command or as an exclamatory sentence. Then ask volunteers to come up to the chart and punctuate the sentences correctly.
- Read aloud the following sentences: *Clean your room. Follow me. This broccoli is delicious! Thank you for everything!* Write the sentences without end punctuation on chart paper. Have students identify the sentences as commands or exclamatory sentences. Have students add the punctuation that goes at the end of each sentence.
- Explain to students the difference between commands and exclamatory sentences. *Commands tell someone what to do and usually end with a period. Exclamatory sentences show strong emotion and end with an exclamation point.*

Extending the Lesson

Ask students to write one command and one exclamatory sentence without end punctuation on a piece of notebook paper. Then have them trade papers with a partner, identify each sentence type, and punctuate the sentences.

On Your Own

Have students write three sentences about school. Tell them to use at least one command and one exclamatory sentence. Ask two volunteers to share their sentences with the class.

You Will Need

- Writer's Handbook, page 36
- chart paper and marker
- paper and pencil for each student

---

1. We're going on a camping trip [exclamatory, exclamation point]
2. Don't forget your backpack [command, period]
3. Put the food in the car [command, period]
4. Hooray, we've arrived [exclamatory, exclamation point]
5. Put up the tent [command, period]
6. We had a great trip [exclamatory, exclamation point]
7. Get out of the water [command, exclamation point]

 Assess Progress

Note whether students understand and can identify imperative and exclamatory sentences. Provide additional practice if necessary.

Review Sentence Types

Lesson Background

A declarative sentence presents facts or ideas and ends with a period. An interrogative sentence asks a question and ends with a question mark. An imperative sentence gives a command and usually ends with a period. An exclamatory sentence shows emotion or surprise and ends with an exclamation point.

Teaching the Lesson

- To review sentence types, read aloud the relevant portions of pages 35–36 of the Writer's Handbook as students follow along.
- Tape the sentence strips to chart paper. Ask volunteers to identify and label each sentence. Then have volunteers add correct end punctuation.
- Give each student four index cards. Have students copy the words *command*, *exclamatory*, *question*, and *statement* onto the cards.
- Read aloud the following sentences and have students hold up the correct index card: *Go to the store.* (command) *The cat is soft.* (statement) *Do you want some pie?* (question) *I always do my homework.* (statement) *I had a great day!* (exclamatory) *Clean your desk.* (command) *How are you?* (question) *Here I come!* (exclamatory) Write each sentence on chart paper, leaving out end punctuation. Then have students identify and add punctuation for each sentence.
- Explain the different sentence types. *A statement tells a fact or an idea and ends with a period. A question asks something and ends with a question mark. A command tells someone to do something and usually ends with a period. An exclamatory sentence shows strong emotion and ends with an exclamation point.*

Extending the Lesson

Draw the chart in the margin on chart paper. Ask volunteers to come up to the chart and fill in the blanks.

On Your Own

Have students write four sentences about an event they enjoyed. Ask them to write one of each sentence type. Encourage students to share their sentences with the class.

Sentence	Sentence Type	End Punctuation
Pick up the pencils		
I love summer		
We are going to visit my aunt this fall		
What will you do when it snows		

✔ Assess Progress

Note whether students are able to differentiate between the four sentence types. Provide additional practice if necessary.

Making Compound Sentences

Lesson Background

A simple sentence expresses one complete thought. A compound sentence contains more than one simple sentence. Two simple sentences can be joined together with a comma and a conjunction, such as *and*, *but*, or *so*, to make a compound sentence.

Teaching the Lesson

- To introduce making compound sentences, read aloud the relevant portion of page 35 of the Writer's Handbook as students follow along. Write the following sentences on chart paper: *I walked the dog. He cleaned the house.* Say *I am going to combine these two simple sentences to create a compound sentence. First I must remove the period from the first sentence and replace it with a comma and a connecting word such as* and. *Then I must make the first letter of the first word of the second sentence lowercase.* Write the completed sentence on chart paper: *I walked the dog, and he cleaned the house.*
- Tape the sentence strips to the board. Tell students that each sentence is made up of two simple sentences joined by a comma and a connecting word, such as *and*, *but*, or *so*. Say *These are compound sentences.*
- Have a volunteer put a box around the connecting word in each sentence. Then have volunteers underline each simple sentence that makes up the compound sentence.
- Explain how to create a compound sentence. *A compound sentence is two simple sentences joined by a comma and a connecting word,* such as and, but or so.

Extending the Lesson

Write the sentences in the margin on chart paper. Have students choose a conjunction and join the simple sentences to make a compound sentence. Remind students to use a comma before the connecting word.

On Your Own

Have students look through books to find examples of compound sentences. Have students write those sentences on a piece of paper. Tell them to underline the simple sentences and put a box around the comma and the connecting word. Then ask students to share their sentences with a partner.

You Will Need

- Writer's Handbook, page 35
- sentence strips with the following sentences written on them:
  Marie dances, and she plays soccer.
  Juan did his homework, but he left it at home.
  Kim finished her chores, so she went to the movies.
- tape
- chart paper and marker
- books for compound sentence examples
- paper and pencil for each student

1. Juliette wants to be a truck driver. Felipe wants to be a teacher. [and/but]
2. Today I have soup and an apple for lunch. I wish I had a sandwich. [but]
3. I am learning to juggle. Wai Man is learning to play the flute and sing. [and]
4. Our pumpkins are ripe. We will make a pie. [and/so]

Assess Progress

Note whether students are able to form compound sentences. Provide additional practice if necessary.

Sentence Combining 1

Lesson Background

Combining short, repetitive simple sentences helps writers vary their sentence length and improve the flow of their writing. This is done by combining related simple sentences to form compound sentences.

Teaching the Lesson

- To introduce combining short, repetitive sentences, read aloud the relevant portion of page 45 of the Writer's Handbook as students follow along.

- Tape the sentence strips to chart paper to form a passage. Read the passage aloud and ask students if the passage sounded smooth or repetitive. (repetitive) Why? (The sentences were short and had a lot of the same information.)

- Ask students how they could combine the first two sentences. (Use the conjunction *and*.) Circle *likes math* in both sentences. Explain that when two sentences have a lot of the same information, you can combine them. Ask students *How could you combine these two sentences?* (*Rosa and Ana like math.*)

- Work with students to combine the other sentences by using conjunctions and write the revised sentences on chart paper. Read the new passage aloud and discuss the difference between the two versions.

- Explain why students should combine short, repetitive sentences. *Short, repetitive sentences are hard to read. Writers should vary the length of their sentences by combining some short sentences to make longer ones. This makes reading more enjoyable and makes your writing sound more like the way people speak.*

Extending the Lesson

Write the sentences in the margin on chart paper. Then have volunteers combine the sentences to make the writing easier to read. Remind students to use connecting words where appropriate.

On Your Own

Have each student choose a piece of writing from his or her writing folder. Then have students trade papers and revise each other's work, focusing on combining short, repetitive sentences.

You Will Need

- Writer's Handbook, page 45
- sentence strips with the following sentences written on them:
  Rosa likes math.
  Ana likes math.
  Math is interesting.
  Math can be hard.
  In class we use rulers.
  We learn how to measure things.
- tape
- paper and pencil for each student
- chart paper and marker

We went on a field trip. We went to a museum. It took a long time to get there. We took a bus. We saw statues. We also saw paintings.

Assess Progress

Note whether students can recognize and combine short, repetitive sentences. Provide additional practice if necessary.

Sentence Combining 2

Lesson Background

A fragment is a group of words that does not express a complete thought. A run-on sentence contains more than one idea but does not contain the necessary conjunction or punctuation between ideas. A rambling sentence contains too many ideas and is not coherent. Students should learn to revise these mistakes using sentence combining.

Teaching the Lesson

- To introduce revising run-on and rambling sentences and fixing sentence fragments, read aloud the relevant portion of page 46 of the Writer's Handbook as students follow along.
- Tape the sentence strips together to the board to form a paragraph. Ask students *Which of these sentences isn't a complete thought? (On a farm.)* Create a new sentence by working with students to complete the thought.
- Ask students *Which of these sentences expresses too many thoughts without correct punctuation or a connecting word? (There are ducks, cows, and horses I like to visit farms.)* Create a revised sentence by working with students to divide up the thoughts with correct punctuation and connecting words.
- Ask students *Which of these sentences is made up of too many short sentences combined with the word* and? *(The farmer plows and workers feed animals and children play and life is peaceful.)* Create a new sentence by working with students to divide up the rambling sentence into shorter, separate sentences.
- Remind students that there are different ways to correct these sentences. Read the new sentences aloud.
- Explain to students why they should revise run-on and rambling sentences and correct sentence fragments. *A sentence needs to be repaired when it does not have proper punctuation between thoughts and when it contains too many different ideas. A fragment needs to be repaired so it expresses a complete thought.*

Extending the Lesson

Write the sentences in the margin on chart paper. Work with students to repair the sentences.

On Your Own

Divide students into pairs. Write the passage called "Doing New Things" on chart paper and have pairs copy it. Have the pairs correct the fragments, run-ons, and rambling sentences in the passage.

You Will Need

- Writer's Handbook, page 46
- sentence strips with the following sentences written on them:
  On a farm. There are ducks, cows, and horses I like to visit farms.
  The farmer plows and workers feed animals and children play and life is peaceful.
- chart paper and marker
- tape
- paper and pencil for each student

---

1. I like to go sledding and I don't like ice skating and do you like to go sledding?
2. My favorite athlete.
3. Tennis is fun I play it in the park.

Doing New Things

Sometimes people get nervous when they are learning new things they can relax and breathe. If you get upset, make a fist and let it go and maybe you just need to learn in a different way. Learning something new.

 **Assess Progress**

Note whether students can identify run-ons, rambling sentences, and sentence fragments. Provide additional practice if necessary.

Theme (6)

Review Sentence Combining

Lesson Background

Students should combine short, repetitive sentences and sentence fragments to make clear, focused sentences. Run-on sentences can be repaired by using punctuation. Rambling sentences need to be broken down into smaller sentences.

Teaching the Lesson

- To review sentence combining, read aloud the relevant portions of pages 35–36 and 45–46 of the Writer's Handbook as students follow along.
- Explain to students that they are now experienced sentence surgeons, or doctors who fix sentences. They can identify sentence structure in need of repair. Tell students that some of their tools are connecting words, such as *and, but,* and *or,* and punctuation.
- Tape the sentence strips to the board. Beneath each strip, write *Identify the problem: _____.* Ask one "surgeon" to come up and identify the problem in the first sentence. Then ask him or her to "operate" on the sentence. Repeat for each sentence.
- Explain to students why they should repair certain sentences. *A sentence should clearly express one idea and have proper punctuation. A sentence needs to be repaired when it does not have proper punctuation between whole thoughts and when it contains too many different ideas. Sentences also need to be combined when they are short and repetitive. Fragments need to be repaired to express a complete thought.*

Extending the Lesson

Write the sentences in the margin on chart paper. Have students find the problem in each sentence and repair it.

On Your Own

Have students choose a piece of writing from their writing folder. Ask them to trade papers with another student. Then have students "operate" on their partner's sentences.

You Will Need

- Writer's Handbook, pages 35–36 and 45–46
- sentence strips with the following sentences written on them:

  Hawaii was the last state to join the United States and it is a nice vacation spot I would like to go there.

  Hawaii is hot. Hawaii has beaches.

  Hawaii is made of islands there are many different kinds of plants and animals there.

  Take trips to Hawaii.

- chart paper and marker
- paper and pencil for each student

---

1. Horses and ponies. Are interesting.

2. Horses use their tail to swat flies they tell other horses how they are feeling with the their tail tails are important to horses.

3. Baby horses are small. Baby horses are interesting.

 **Assess Progress**

Note whether students can recognize and fix rambling sentences, run-ons, short, repetitive sentences, and sentence fragments. Provide additional practice if necessary.

Common Nouns

Lesson Background

A common noun names a general person, place, thing, or idea. Common nouns begin with a lowercase letter.

Teaching the Lesson

- To review common nouns, read aloud the relevant portion of page 20 of the Writer's Handbook as students follow along.
- Write the words *cat, playground, lamp, happiness, city,* and *teacher* on chart paper. Ask students to identify what these words have in common. Tell students that these words are called common nouns because they name general people, places, things, or ideas.
- Point out that common nouns begin with a lowercase letter because they do not name a specific person, place, thing, or idea.
- Copy the chart from the margin onto chart paper. Have students suggest as many words as they can for each column. To get students started, suggest *firefighter, school, truck,* and *peace.*
- Read from a book four sentences with common nouns. Ask students to raise their hand whenever they hear a common noun. Add these words to the chart.
- Explain to students how to identify and use common nouns. *A common noun names a general person, place, thing, or idea. Common nouns begin with a lowercase letter.*

Extending the Lesson

Tell students that some people, places, things, or ideas may be referred to by more than one common noun. Explain that you are a teacher. The word *teacher* is a common noun. Then mention another noun that could refer to you, such as *parent, driver,* or *writer.* Have each student write down three common nouns that could refer to him or her.

On Your Own

Have students expand their lists of nouns and make word webs with them. Use the example below as a guide.

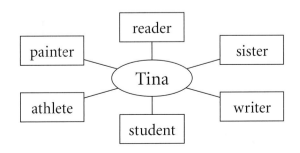

People	Places	Things	Ideas

Assess Progress

Note whether students are able to identify and use common nouns. Provide additional practice if necessary.

Proper Nouns

Lesson Background

Unlike a common noun, a proper noun names a specific person, place, thing, or idea. Proper nouns begin with a capital letter.

Teaching the Lesson

- To review proper nouns, read aloud the relevant portion of page 20 of the Writer's Handbook as students follow along.
- Write the words *Mexico, Atlanta, Washington Monument,* and *Benjamin Franklin* on chart paper. Tell students that these words are proper nouns because they name specific people, places, or things. Point out that proper nouns begin with a capital letter.
- Have students look through books that you have in the classroom to find examples of proper nouns. Ask students to list on notebook paper five proper nouns they find in the books.
- Explain to students how to identify and use proper nouns. *Proper nouns name certain people, places, or things. Every proper noun always begins with a capital letter.*

Extending the Lesson

Copy the sentences from the margin onto chart paper. Have students identify the proper nouns and ask them to properly capitalize each one.

On Your Own

List the following nouns on the board: the name of your school's principal, the capital city of your state, the name of another teacher, the name of your town, and a holiday in lowercase letters. Ask students to write sentences using the words on the board, making sure to capitalize all proper nouns. Then have volunteers share their sentences with the class.

You Will Need

- Writer's Handbook, page 20
- chart paper and marker
- paper and pencil for each student
- books for examples of proper nouns

1. My mother and audrey threw a surprise party for bill. [Audrey, Bill]

2. I went to san diego and portland for summer vacation. [San Diego, Portland]

3. My friend saw the declaration of independence on her trip to washington, d.c. [Declaration of Independence; Washington, D.C.]

4. ms. rosser works at a store called tianna's tasty treats. [Ms. Rosser, Tianna's Tasty Treats]

 **Assess Progress**

Note whether students are able to identify, use, and capitalize proper nouns. Provide additional practice if necessary.

Singular and Plural Nouns

Lesson Background

A noun names a person, place, thing, or idea. Nouns can be singular or plural. A singular noun names only one person, place, thing, or idea. A plural noun names more than one person, place, thing, or idea. Most plurals are made by adding -s or -es, but some plurals are irregular.

Teaching the Lesson

- To introduce singular and plural nouns, read aloud the relevant portion of page 20 of the Writer's Handbook as students follow along.

- Draw a T-chart on chart paper. Label the left side *Singular* and the right side *Plural*. Tape the index cards in the *Singular* column. Explain that these are called singular nouns because they name just one person, place, thing, or idea.

- Explain that for most words, students should add just an -s to the end of the singular form to make the plural. Tell students that for words that end in a consonant and -y, they should change the -y to i and add -es. Nouns that end in -sh, -ch, -ss, or -x have -es added to them in the plural form. For words that end in a consonant plus an o, students should add -es.

- Tell students that some nouns can be irregular and don't follow the patterns. Write the following sentence on chart paper: *The child ran home.* Say *If we change* child *from the singular to the plural form, it becomes* children. *This pattern does not follow the rules we've discussed about plural and singular nouns.*

- Work with students to form plurals of the nouns in the *Singular* column of the T-chart. Have volunteers write the plural nouns on index cards and tape them in the *Plural* column.

- Explain how to make plurals. *Plural nouns are formed by adding* -s *or* -es *to the end of the singular noun most of the time. Irregular nouns follow different rules and their plural forms must be memorized.*

Extending the Lesson

Divide students into groups. Ask groups to write down as many animals as they can name in two minutes. Then ask groups to read their lists and write down both the singular and plural forms of the nouns. Have them share with the class. Deal with irregular plurals on a case-by-case basis.

On Your Own

Divide students into pairs. Have partners look through books you have in the classroom and ask them to make a list of ten singular nouns. Then have them change these singular nouns into their plural forms.

You Will Need

- Writer's Handbook, page 20
- chart paper and marker
- index cards with the following words written on them: *bottle, dog, man, student, store, dish, box, fox, kiss, bench, goose*
- tape
- books for singular noun examples
- eleven blank index cards
- paper and pencil for each student

Assess Progress

Note whether students are able to form singular and plural nouns. Provide additional practice if necessary.

Theme ⑧
Singular/Plural Possessive Nouns

Lesson Background

An apostrophe can show possession. Most singular possessives end with an apostrophe and -s. (Dave's hat, Sadie's dog) If a noun has more than one syllable and ends in an -s, it takes only an apostrophe. (Dallas' population) If a noun is plural, place the apostrophe after the -s. Plurals that don't end in an -s take an apostrophe plus an -s.

Teaching the Lesson

- To introduce singular and plural possessive nouns, read aloud the relevant portion of page 19 of the Writer's Handbook as students follow along.
- Explain that a possessive noun shows who owns something. Tape the sentence strip to the board. Say *Marta's is the possessive noun because Marta owns something—the book.* Note the apostrophe and -s.
- Explain that sometimes more than one person or thing can own an object. Write the following two phrases on chart paper: *the girl _____ mother, the girls _____ mother.*
- Circle *girl* and say *This is one girl because the noun* girl *is singular.* Add an apostrophe and -s. If possible, draw a picture of a mother and one girl to illustrate the phrase.
- Circle *girls* and say *This is more than one girl because the noun* girls *is plural.* Add an apostrophe after the -s. If possible, draw a picture of a mother and two girls to illustrate the phrase.
- Tell students that some nouns are irregular and have plural forms that look different than the singular form. Write the following sentence on chart paper: *The child's cat wanted more milk.* Ask students what possessive noun could be used if there were more than one child. (*children's*)
- Explain how to make possessives. *Most singular nouns are made possessive by adding an apostrophe and -s. Many plural nouns take only an apostrophe at the end of the word. Plural nouns that don't end in an -s take an apostrophe plus -s.*

Extending the Lesson

Write the phrases in the margin on chart paper. Have students choose one set and draw a picture to show whether each phrase they chose is singular or plural.

On Your Own

Copy the sentences in the margin onto chart paper. Have students copy these onto their own paper. Tell them to fill in the blank with the correct possessive noun.

You Will Need

- Writer's Handbook, page 19
- sentence strip with the following sentence written on it: *Marta's book is green.*
- chart paper and marker
- paper and pencil for each student
- tape

1. farmer's cows / farmers' cows
2. bee's hive / bees' hive
3. dog's house / dogs' house

1. My _____ name is John. (father) [father's]
2. My _____ cat is black. (friend) [friend's]
3. _____ house is on the way to the park. (Jen and Rylan) [Jen and Rylan's]
4. The _____ soccer team won the game. (men) [men's]
5. Our _____ bikes are new. (cousins) [cousins']
6. The _____ bowls are empty. (cats) [cats']

 **Assess Progress**

Note whether students can identify and form plural and singular possessives. Provide additional practice if necessary.

16 *Theme 8*   *Singular/Plural Possessive Nouns*

Contractions

Lesson Background

A contraction is the shortened form of two words that are put together. An apostrophe is used to take the place of the missing letter or letters. A new word, called a contraction, is formed.

Teaching the Lesson

- To review contractions, read aloud the relevant portion of page 18 of the Writer's Handbook as students follow along.
- Tape the index cards with the words *is* and *not* onto the board. Have a volunteer read the words. Have another volunteer use the words in a sentence.
- Put the cards together on the board. Cover the *o* in *not* with the apostrophe card. Ask a student to read the new word. (*isn't*) Tell students that when you combine two words into one using an apostrophe in place of one or more letters, you make a contraction.
- Draw a T-chart on chart paper. Label the left column *Two Words* and the right column *Contraction*. Write *do not, I am,* and *was not* in the first column. Work with students to combine these words to form contractions. Write the new words in the second column. Explain that the contraction has the same meaning as the two words. Remind students that they should use contractions only in informal writing.
- Ask students to add other contractions they know to the list. Ask them to fill in the *Two Words* column. Then have students determine the contraction. Emphasize how the sounds blend together and sometimes change.
- Explain how contractions are formed. *A contraction is a shortened form of two words. An apostrophe replaces the letter or letters in the original words.*

Extending the Lesson

Write the sentences from the margin on chart paper. For each sentence, have students identify the words they can make into contractions and circle them. Tape a blank index card over these words. Have a volunteer write the new word on the index card.

On Your Own

Divide students into groups. Give each group a set of index cards and have them write the following on them: *D, I, D, N, O, T,* and an apostrophe. Ask groups to use the cards with letters to spell out two words. (*did not*) Then have the groups use the apostrophe to replace a letter and make a contraction. (*didn't*) Have the group make three new sets of contraction cards following the same pattern.

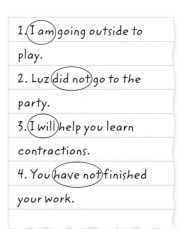

1. (I am) going outside to play.

2. Luz (did not) go to the party.

3. (I will) help you learn contractions.

4. You (have not) finished your work.

 Assess Progress

Note whether students can identify and form contractions. Provide additional practice if necessary.

Pronouns and Antecedents

Lesson Background

The antecedent of a pronoun is the word, phrase, or clause to which a pronoun refers. Antecedents and pronouns must agree in number. For example, if the antecedent is singular, the pronoun must also be singular.

Teaching the Lesson

- To introduce pronouns and antecedents, read aloud the relevant portion of page 22 of the Writer's Handbook as students follow along.
- Write the following sentence on chart paper: *Eva lost her homework.* Have a volunteer underline the noun (*Eva*) and the pronoun. (*her*) Tell students that the pronoun *her* refers to the noun *Eva*. Say *When we use a pronoun to refer to a noun in a sentence, we must make sure that the noun and pronoun agree in number. Eva is one person, so we must use the singular pronoun* her.
- Write the following sentence below the first sentence: *Teachers take care of their students.* Have a volunteer underline the pronoun in the sentence (*their*) and the noun it refers to. (*Teachers*) Say *In this sentence the pronoun* their *refers to the noun* teachers. *Because* teachers *is a plural noun, we must use a plural pronoun.* (their)
- Write the following sentence on chart paper: *Jean and Ben went to the zoo because _____ like animals.* Have a volunteer fill in the blank. Tell students that we use the pronoun *they* to refer to the nouns *Jean* and *Ben*.
- Explain pronouns and antecedents to students. *A pronoun can refer to a word or phrase that is in a sentence. These pronouns and words and phrases must agree in number.*

Extending the Lesson

Write the sentences from the margin on chart paper. Have students copy them onto their own papers. For each sentence, have students fill in the correct pronoun.

On Your Own

Have students look through books from the classroom for pronouns and the words and phrases to which they refer. Have students write down the sentences and circle the pronouns and underline the words and phrases to which they refer.

1. <u>Our class</u> went to a police station because ____ were studying jobs. [we]
2. <u>The police officers</u> looked tough, but ____ were very kind. [they]
3. When <u>our class</u> finished talking to the police officers, ____ met ambulance drivers. [we]
4. <u>My friend Jane</u> liked the trip. ____ said that ____ wants to be a police officer when ____ grows up. [She/she/she]

Assess Progress

Note whether students can match pronouns with antecedents. Provide additional practice if necessary.

Singular and Plural Pronouns

Lesson Background

A pronoun replaces a noun. Pronouns can be singular or plural. Singular pronouns refer to only one person, place, or thing and include *I, you, he, she, it, me, him,* and *her.* They replace singular nouns. Plural pronouns refer to two or more people, places, or things and include *we, you, they, us,* and *them.* They replace plural nouns.

Teaching the Lesson

- To review singular and plural pronouns, read aloud the relevant portion of page 22 of the Writer's Handbook as students follow along.
- Write the following sentence on chart paper: *She brought colored pencils to class.* Circle *She.* Ask *How many people is this?* (one) Write *singular.* Write *They played tetherball.* Circle *They.* Ask *How many people is this?* (more than one) Write *plural.*
- Write the following sentence on chart paper: *I like potatoes.* Ask *How many people like potatoes in this sentence?* (one) Write *singular.* Write *My sisters, my grandmother, and I like green peppers.* Explain to students that the word *we* can replace the series of nouns in this sentence. Write *We like green peppers.* Ask *How many people is this?* (more than one) Write *plural.*
- Write *You like recess.* Ask students to change the pronoun from singular to plural. Tell them that this one is tricky. Point to two students in the class. Say *You like recess, and you like recess. If I put them together, I can say* You like recess. *The word* you *can be both singular and plural.*
- Tell students that pronouns do not always refer to people. Write the following sentence on chart paper: *They ran in the forest.* Say *The word* They *can refer to a group of animals. The word* They *is also a plural pronoun.*
- Explain the difference between singular and plural pronouns. *Singular pronouns tell about only one person, place, or thing and replace singular nouns. Plural pronouns tell about two or more people, places, or things and replace plural nouns.*

Extending the Lesson

Divide students into pairs. Copy the list in the margin onto chart paper. Have students write the pronouns on index cards and sort them into stacks of singular and plural pronouns. Then have students write sentences using each pronoun.

On Your Own

Have students write three sentences about what they do on the weekend. Tell them to use pronouns in their sentences. Then ask students to identify the pronouns as singular or plural.

You Will Need

- Writer's Handbook, page 22
- chart paper and marker
- paper and pencil for each student
- 12 index cards for each student

I	me
we	him
you	her
he	us
she	them
it	
they	

Assess Progress

Note whether students can identify singular and plural pronouns and use them correctly. Provide additional practice if necessary.

Theme ⑩

Subject/Object Pronouns

Lesson Background

Pronouns include both subject pronouns and object pronouns. Subject pronouns include *I, you, he, she, it, we,* and *they.* An object pronoun (*me, you, him, her, it, us,* and *them*) is used as the object of a verb or as the object of a prepositional phrase.

Teaching the Lesson

- To review subject and object pronouns, read aloud the relevant portion of page 22 of the Writer's Handbook as students follow along.
- Toss a beanbag in the air and catch it. Then write the following sentence on chart paper: *I caught it.* Circle the pronoun *I.* Explain that *I* is the subject pronoun because that is the person doing the action. Draw a box around the word *it.* Say *The word* it *is the object pronoun because it names something the action happens to.*
- Toss the beanbag to a boy in your class. Then write on chart paper *I threw him the beanbag.* Ask students to identify the subject pronoun. Remind them that the subject performs the action in a sentence. Circle *I.* Ask students to identify the object pronoun. Draw a box around *him.*
- Have the student toss the beanbag back. Write *He threw a beanbag to me.* Ask students to identify the subject pronoun. Circle *He.* Have students identify the object pronoun. Draw a box around *me* and point out that *me* is the object of a preposition.
- Explain subject and object pronouns. *A subject pronoun is a pronoun that performs the action in the sentence. An object pronoun is a pronoun that is the object of a verb or a preposition.*

Extending the Lesson

Copy the sentences in the margin onto chart paper. Have volunteers choose the correct pronoun. Then have volunteers circle the pronoun if it is a subject pronoun and draw a box around it if it is an object pronoun.

On Your Own

Divide students into pairs. Have them look through fiction and nonfiction books in the classroom and find two sentences with subject and object pronouns. Have them copy the sentences and then circle the subject pronouns and put a box around the object pronouns.

1. (I/Me) enjoy going on hikes.
2. Mom gave (her/she) new hiking boots.
3. I threw (him/he) the football.
4. (We/Us) found a rock at the park.
5. (He/Him) bought tickets for (them/they) last week.

Assess Progress

Note whether students can identify subject and object pronouns. Provide additional practice if necessary.

Theme (11)
Adjectives

Lesson Background
Adjectives are words that describe nouns or pronouns.

Teaching the Lesson
- To review adjectives, read aloud the relevant portion of page 26 of the Writer's Handbook as students follow along.
- Show students three objects, such as a book, a ball, and a pencil. On chart paper, write *It is blue. It is round.* Ask students to guess which object you are describing. Underline *blue* and *round.* Explain that these words are adjectives that describe the ball. Say *An adjective describes a noun. It can describe how something looks, feels, smells, tastes, or sounds.*
- Write *The red book is on the table.* Ask students to identify the adjective in this sentence. (*red*) Ask students to think of another sentence that describes the book. Write the sentence on chart paper and have students identify the adjective.
- Ask a student to describe the book, ball, or pencil without telling the rest of the class which object he or she is describing. Write the description on chart paper. Underline the adjectives and have students decide which object the student is describing.
- Repeat with other objects in the classroom, as time allows.
- Explain adjectives. *An adjective describes a noun or a pronoun. It can tell how a noun looks, feels, smells, tastes, or sounds.*

Extending the Lesson
Show students a bag with a mystery object inside. Ask a volunteer to feel the object without looking into the bag and use adjectives to describe it to the class. Write the adjectives on chart paper. Then have students guess what the mystery object is.

On Your Own
Copy the paragraph in the margin onto chart paper. Have students copy it onto their paper and underline the adjectives. Then have students complete the last sentence with appropriate adjectives.

You Will Need
- Writer's Handbook, page 26
- a red book, a blue ball, and a pencil
- chart paper and marker
- bag with mystery object inside such as an eraser or marker.
- paper and pencil for each student

In my home, there is a big, soft chair. I like to read my favorite books in the comfortable chair. My little sister turns the chair into a big fort. The chair makes me feel _____ and _____.

Assess Progress
Note whether students can identify and use adjectives correctly. Provide additional practice if necessary.

Theme ⑪
Comparative and Superlative Adjectives

You Will Need
- Writer's Handbook, page 27
- one thick picture book, one thicker chapter book, and one very thick book, such as a dictionary
- chart paper and marker
- paper and pencil for each student

Lesson Background

Adjectives describe nouns or pronouns. Comparative adjectives compare two people, places, things, or ideas. The suffix *-er* is added to these adjectives when they have one syllable. You can add *more* before an adjective with two or more syllables. Superlative adjectives compare three or more people, places, things, or ideas. The suffix *-est* is added to these adjectives when they have one syllable. You can add *most* before an adjective that has two or more syllables.

Teaching the Lesson

- To review comparative and superlative adjectives, read aloud the relevant portion of page 27 of the Writer's Handbook as students follow along.
- Show students a thick picture book. On chart paper, write the following sentence: *This book is thick.* Then show students a chapter book and write *This book is thicker.* Finally, show a very thick book like a dictionary and write *This book is the thickest.* Ask students to identify the adjectives. (*thick, thicker, thickest*) Underline them.
- Say *The word* thick *is an adjective. It describes the noun* book. Thicker *is an adjective that compares two things. You add the word part* -er *to compare two things.* Thickest *is also an adjective. You add the word part* -est *to the word* thick *to compare three or more things.*
- Tell students that words with three or more syllables take *more* or *most* before the adjective. Some two syllable words also follow this pattern.
- Choose other objects in the classroom to compare. On chart paper, write sentences using adjectives with *-er* and *-est* or *more* or *most* for longer adjectives.
- Explain comparative and superlative adjectives. *An adjective with the ending* -er *compares two things, and an adjective that has the* -est *ending compares three or more things. You can add* more *or* most *before longer adjectives.*

Extending the Lesson

Write the paragraph in the margin on chart paper and read it aloud. Have students copy it onto their own paper. Then have students identify the comparative and superlative adjectives by circling them.

On Your Own

Have students compare the heights of three people they know. Tell them to draw a picture showing the heights of the three people. Then have students write a sentence below each picture using adjectives, including an *-er* adjective and an *-est* adjective. (*e.g., tall, taller, tallest*)

> Coins come in different sizes. A quarter is big, but there are (larger) coins. A half-dollar is (bigger) than a quarter. A nickel is small, but a penny is (smaller). A dime is the (smallest) coin of all.

✓ Assess Progress

Note whether students can recognize and use comparative and superlative adjectives. Provide additional practice if necessary.

Articles

Lesson Background

Articles include the words *a, an,* and *the.* There are two types of articles: definite and indefinite. The word *the* is a definite article because it signals a specific noun. The words *a* and *an* are indefinite articles. They do not specify which noun.

Teaching the Lesson

- To introduce articles, read aloud the tip on page 26 of the Writer's Handbook as students follow along.
- On chart paper write the following sentence: *The farmer planted a potato.* Underline the words *The* and *a.* Explain that these are articles.
- Tell students there are two kinds of articles: definite and indefinite. *The* is a definite article because it tells which farmer. *A* and *an* are indefinite articles. The word *a* does not show which potato the farmer planted.
- Instruct students that the word *a* is used before a noun that begins with a consonant and the word *an* comes before a noun that begins with a vowel.
- Write the following sentence on chart paper: *The child picked an apple.* Have a volunteer underline the articles. (*The* and *an*) Have the students explain what kinds of articles these words are.
- Explain articles to students. *The words* a, an, *and* the *are articles. There are two kinds of articles: definite and indefinite.* A *and* an *are indefinite and* the *is definite.*

Extending the Lesson

Write the paragraph from the margin on chart paper and read it aloud. Have students identify and circle the articles. Then have them label each article as definite or indefinite.

On Your Own

Write these sentences on chart paper: *I went to the movie with _____ friend. A spider is not _____ insect, but it is _____ arachnid. Mom wants _____ original album she had as a child.* Ask students to copy these sentences onto their own paper and fill in the blanks with the correct articles.

You Will Need

- Writer's Handbook, page 26
- chart paper and marker
- paper and pencil for each student

(A)fossa is(an)animal that lives on(the)small island of Madagascar. It looks like (a)cat with(an)extremely long tail. Not many people have seen(the)fossa. It lives deep in(the)forest, hiding during(the)day and hunting at night.

Assess Progress

Note whether students can identify and use articles. Provide additional practice if necessary.

Theme ⑫
Review Adjectives

Lesson Background

An adjective describes a noun or a pronoun. A comparative adjective compares one noun to another. A superlative adjective compares a noun to two or more nouns. Articles are also adjectives.

Teaching the Lesson

- To review adjectives, read aloud the relevant portions of pages 26–27 of the Writer's Handbook as students follow along.
- On chart paper, write the following riddle: *What time is it when an elephant sits on a wooden fence?* Underline *an*, *a*, and *wooden*. Tell students that the articles *a* and *an* and the word *wooden* are adjectives.
- Write the following answer: *It's time to get a new fence!* Have students identify the article and adjective. (*a*, *new*)
- Now write *Maya's riddle is funnier, but Caleb's riddle is the funniest.* Underline *funnier* and *funniest*. Remind students that *funnier* and *funniest* are adjectives that compare and *an* is an article.
- Ask students to create sentences using *old*, *older*, and *oldest*. Write the sentences on chart paper. Identify and underline the adjectives, including the articles.
- Explain the different adjective forms. *Adjectives describe nouns or pronouns. Adjectives can also compare nouns. The articles* a, an, *and* the *are also adjectives.*

Extending the Lesson

Copy the paragraph "My Favorite Toy" from the margin onto chart paper. Have volunteers underline the adjectives. Then ask students to write three sentences about their own favorite toy or game, using as many adjectives as they can. When students are done, have them exchange papers with a partner and underline the adjectives.

On Your Own

Have students look in books for examples of adjectives. Ask them to write one example of each kind of adjective on separate index cards. Have them write their names on the cards as well. Then have students place the index cards into the appropriate shoebox.

You Will Need

- Writer's Handbook, pages 26–27
- chart paper and marker
- paper and pencil for each student.
- four blank index cards for each student
- books for examples of adjectives
- four shoeboxes, each with one of the following labels: *adjective*, *article*, -er *adjective*, -est *adjective*

My Favorite Toy

This <u>stuffed</u> elephant is my <u>favorite</u> toy. It is <u>gray</u>, <u>fuzzy</u>, and <u>soft</u>. I was given <u>the</u> elephant when I was <u>a</u> <u>little</u> baby. It was <u>bigger</u> than I was then. It is still <u>the</u> <u>biggest</u> <u>stuffed</u> animal I have. <u>An</u> elephant is <u>a</u> <u>great</u> toy. You can pretend it lives in <u>the</u> zoo or travels with <u>a</u> <u>famous</u> circus.

Assess Progress

Note whether students can identify and write sentences with different kinds of adjectives. Provide additional practice if necessary.

Action and Linking Verbs

Lesson Background

Action verbs show what the subject of a sentence is doing. Linking verbs link the subject to a noun or adjective in the predicate.

Teaching the Lesson

- To review action and linking verbs, read aloud the relevant portions of pages 23–24 of the Writer's Handbook as students follow along.
- Read the following sentences aloud: *Toni stirred the spaghetti sauce.* Have students identify the verb in the sentence. Say *Toni is performing an action, so* stirred *is an action verb.* Circle *stirred.*
- Read the following sentence aloud: *The cat is hungry.* Have students identify the verb in this sentence. (*is*) Say *There is no action in this sentence.* Explain that the word *hungry* describes the cat. The linking verb *is* links *cat* to *hungry.* Underline *is.*
- On chart paper, create a T-chart like the one in the margin. Label one column *Action Verbs* and the other column *Linking Verbs.* Tape the sentence strips next to the chart. Ask students to write the verbs from each sentence strip in the appropriate column.
- Explain to students that all sentences contain a verb. *If the verb shows the subject performing an action, it is an action verb. If the verb links the subject to a noun or an adjective in the predicate, it is a linking verb.*

Extending the Lesson

Ask students to brainstorm five verbs. Write each verb on an index card, and then tape it next to the chart from the previous activity. Ask volunteers to come forward and place each index card in the correct column.

On Your Own

Have students write a few sentences about what they do when they get home from school. Have them circle all the verbs in their sentences. Then have students label each verb by writing an *A* above action verbs and an *L* above linking verbs.

You Will Need

- Writer's Handbook, pages 23–24
- sentence strips with the following sentences written on them:
  Pasta is my favorite food.
  The kitten licked her paws.
  Lemons seem sour.
  The chef prepared soup.
  I am a good student.
- tape
- chart paper and marker
- paper and pencil for each student
- blank index cards

Action Verbs	Linking Verbs
[licked]	[is]
[prepared]	[seem]
	[am]

Assess Progress

Note whether students are able to identify action verbs and linking verbs. Provide additional practice if necessary.

Main and Helping Verbs

Lesson Background

Some sentences contain a main verb and a helping verb. The main verb describes the action the subject performs. The helping verb assists the main verb and can help show when the action takes place.

Teaching the Lesson

- To introduce main and helping verbs, read aloud the relevant portions of pages 23–24 of the Writer's Handbook as students follow along.
- Read the following sentence aloud: *Monique is eating celery sticks.* Identify the verbs. Explain that *eating* is the main verb because it shows action. Tell students that the word *is* is also a verb. It is the helping verb because it helps the main verb show when the action takes place. The word *is* shows us the action is happening right now.
- Read the following sentence to students: *The cat was sleeping in the window.* Ask students to identify the main verb and the helping verb. (*sleeping, was*) Then have them identify whether the action is in the past, present, or future. Explain that the helping verb can help show the time when the action happens.
- Explain main and helping verbs to students. *The main verb shows the action in a sentence, and the helping verb can help the main verb show when the action takes place.*

Extending the Lesson

Write the sentences from the margin on chart paper. Have students copy the sentences onto their own paper. Tell them to circle the main verbs and underline the helping verbs.

On Your Own

Have students look through books or magazines to find main and helping verbs. Have them write three examples of sentences that contain both types of verbs and then share the sentences with a partner.

You Will Need

- Writer's Handbook, pages 23–24
- chart paper and marker
- paper and pencil for each student
- books or magazines with examples of main and helping verbs

1. We are playing a game.
   [are playing]

2. Aki is asking for help.
   [is asking]

3. They will eat outside.
   [will eat]

4. Mark has taken his turn.
   [has taken]

 Assess Progress

Note whether students are able to identify main verbs and helping verbs. Provide additional practice if necessary.

Present and Past Tense

Lesson Background

The present tense of a verb expresses action happening now. The two main forms of the present tense are simple present (*He jumps*) and present continuous. (*He is jumping*) The past tense of a verb expresses action that has already happened. The main form of the past tense is the simple past. (*He jumped*)

Teaching the Lesson

- To review past and present tense, read aloud the relevant portion of page 26 of the Writer's Handbook as students follow along.
- Write the following sentences on chart paper: *José walked home from school. Then he started his homework.* Read the sentences aloud. Ask students to identify the verbs. (*walked, started*) Circle *walked* and *started*. Say *The verbs* walked *and* started *show that the action happened in the past. These verbs are in the past tense.*
- Read the following sentences aloud: *José climbs a wall. José plays outside.* Explain that the words *climbs* and *plays* show action that is happening now. These verbs are in the present tense.
- Explain how to use present tense and past tense. *Present tense shows action that is happening now. Past tense shows action that has already happened.*

Extending the Lesson

Copy the paragraph from the margin onto chart paper. Ask students to identify the verbs. Underline the verbs as students identify them. Together, rewrite the paragraph so it is in the past tense.

On Your Own

Ask students to think of a time they did something well. Have students write three sentences about that time. Remind students that since the action already happened, all their sentences should be in the past tense.

You Will Need

- Writer's Handbook, page 26
- chart paper and marker
- paper and pencil for each student

Billy <u>practices</u> basketball every day. He <u>drinks</u> plenty of water. He also <u>practices</u> soccer and <u>rides</u> his bike. Billy <u>enjoys</u> all of these activities.

Assess Progress

Note whether students are able to identify past and present tense. Provide additional practice if necessary.

Future Tense

Lesson Background

The future tense of a verb shows action that has not yet happened. The main form of the future tense is simple future. (*He will jump* or *He is going to jump*)

Teaching the Lesson

- To introduce future tense, read aloud the relevant portion of page 26 of the Writer's Handbook as students follow along.

- Ask students to name things they think will happen tomorrow. Write several of the responses on chart paper. Make sure the verb is in the future tense. (for example, *am going to play*, *may take a nap*, and *will eat*) Point out that each verb tells an action that will happen in the future. This means that the action is in the future tense. Tell students that the future tense can be formed by adding a helping verb.

- After students respond, say *These actions are in the future tense. They have not happened yet, and they are not happening now. They will happen in the future.*

- On chart paper, write the following sentence: *Kim _____ go to summer camp next year.* Tell students that because the future is unknown, there are several ways of saying this. Demonstrate this by taping one of the index cards over the blank and discussing its meaning in the sentence. Repeat with the rest of the index cards.

- Explain the future tense. *Future tense describes an action that has not yet happened but is expected to happen in the future.*

Extending the Lesson

Copy the sentences in the margin onto chart paper. Have students fill in a helping verb to create future verb tense. Discuss their responses.

On Your Own

Ask students to write three sentences that tell what they will do next weekend. Have them underline all the verbs, both helping and main, in the paragraph. Remind them that all the verbs used should be in the future tense.

You Will Need

- Writer's Handbook, page 26
- chart paper and marker
- index cards with the following words written on them: *will*, *may*, and *is going to*
- tape
- paper and pencil for each student

1. Lin and Carmen _____ play baseball next year.
2. The cat _____ climb a tree.
3. That woman _____ be a great singer.

Assess Progress

Note whether students are able to identify and use the future tense. Provide additional practice if necessary.

Irregular Verbs

Lesson Background

Most regular verbs in the past tense can be formed by adding *-ed* to the end of the word. Irregular verbs can be challenging for students because they do not follow this pattern. Students must learn each irregular verb.

Teaching the Lesson

- To review irregular verbs, read aloud the relevant portions of pages 24–25 of the Writer's Handbook as students follow along.
- Write the following word on chart paper: *go*. Tell students that you are now going to use this word to write a sentence in the present tense. Write *I go to school.* Explain that this sentence is in the present tense because it is happening now.
- Next write *I went to school.* Tell students that this sentence is in the past tense because it already happened. Note that the word *go* is irregular and the past tense is not formed with *-ed*.
- On chart paper, copy the headings from the margin. Work with students to place the verbs *goes* and *went* in the appropriate columns.
- Tape the sentence strips to the board. Have students use the list on page 25 of their Writer's Handbook to help them change each sentence into the past tense.
- Explain to students how to recognize irregular verbs. *You cannot form the past tense of an irregular verb by adding* -ed. *Sometimes the past tense of an irregular verb looks very different from its present tense.*

Extending the Lesson

Read the following verbs aloud to the class: *do, eat, fall, forget, get, fly.* Add the verbs to the chart you made in the last activity. As a class, complete the chart by changing each of the irregular verbs you read into its past tense form.

On Your Own

Add the verbs in the chart that is in the margin to your class chart. Have students copy the chart onto their own paper and fill in the missing verb tense forms in each column.

Present Tense	Past Tense
	drove
	began
	rode
shake	
throw	
wear	

Assess Progress

Note whether students are able to identify and use irregular verbs. Provide additional practice if necessary.

Theme 15

Review All Verbs

Lesson Background

Action verbs show the action a subject performs. Linking verbs connect the subject to a noun or adjective in the predicate. Helping verbs work with the main verb to show tense or time. The tense of a verb shows if an action occurred in the past, is occurring in the present, or will occur in the future. Irregular verbs do not follow regular rules for forming the past tense.

Teaching the Lesson

- To review verbs, read aloud the relevant portions of pages 23–26 of the Writer's Handbook as students follow along.
- Tape the chart paper with the verb category list to the board.
- Tape up the first sentence strip. Have students underline the verb in the sentence. (*is*) Say *What tense is it?* (present) Ask *Is it an action or linking verb?* (linking) Ask students to explain linking verbs in their own words.
- Tape up the second sentence strip. Ask students to underline the verb. (*went*) Say *What tense is it?* (past) Say *Is it an action verb or a linking verb?* (action) Ask students to explain an action verb in their own words. Say *Is the verb regular or irregular?* (irregular)
- Tape up the third sentence strip. Have a volunteer underline the verb. (*will visit*) Say *Which is the main verb?* (*visit*) Circle *will*. Remind students that *will* is a helping verb because it helps show when something happened. Say *What tense is this verb?* (future) Say *Is the verb regular or irregular?* (regular)
- Review the types of verbs. *An action verb describes what the subject is doing. A linking verb connects the subject to a noun or adjective in the predicate. Main verbs tell the main action, and helping verbs help the main verb show when the action takes place. Present, past, and future tenses show the time of the action. Irregular verbs do not add* -ed *in order to form the past tense.*

Extending the Lesson

Copy the sentences from the margin onto chart paper. Have students fill in the blanks with the correct tense of the verb in parentheses.

On Your Own

Have students look through books for an example of an action verb, a helping verb, a linking verb, and an irregular verb. Have students list and label the examples they find. Then have students work in pairs to check their verbs.

You Will Need

- Writer's Handbook, pages 23–26
- chart paper and marker
- Chart paper with the following verb categories written on it: *action, linking, helping, main, irregular, past tense, present tense,* and *future tense.*
- sentence strips with the following sentences written on them:
  1. *The jungle is a beautiful place.*
  2. *I went there last year.*
  3. *I will visit Africa again.*
- tape
- books for verb examples
- paper and pencil for each student

---

1. The class ____ on a field trip tomorrow. (go) [will go]
2. I always ____ both ways before I cross a street. (look) [look]
3. The giraffe ____ leaves from that tree yesterday. (eat) [ate]
4. I ____ my homework before I started to read my book. (finish) [finished]
5. I ____ that picture and gave it to my mom. (draw) [drew]

 Assess Progress

Note whether students are able to identify and use different verb types and tenses. Provide additional practice if necessary.

Adverbs

Lesson Background

An adverb tells how, where, or when an action is performed. Many adverbs can be formed by adding the suffix *-ly* to an adjective. Adverbs can describe verbs, adjectives, or other adverbs. This lesson will focus on adverbs that modify verbs.

Teaching the Lesson

- To introduce adverbs, read the relevant portion of page 27 of the Writer's Handbook as students follow along.
- Read the following sentence aloud and write it on chart paper: *Sheng put the books there.* Ask *Where did Sheng put the books?* Underline *there.* Explain that the word *there* is an adverb because it tells where. Tell students that *there* describes the verb *put.*
- Read the following sentence aloud and write it on chart paper: *Leila called me today.* Ask *When did Leila call?* Underline *today.* Say *The word* today *is an adverb because it answers when.* Tell students that *today* describes the verb *called.*
- Read the following sentence aloud and write it on chart paper: *Joseph spoke softly.* Ask *How did Joseph speak?* Underline *softly.* Say *The word* softly *is an adverb because it answers how. The word* softly *describes* spoke.
- Write the following words on the board: *quickly, suddenly, kindly.* Ask students what these words have in common. (They end in *-ly.*) Tell students that many adverbs end in the word part *-ly.*
- Explain to students the definition of adverbs. *Adverbs tell how, where, or when an action happens. They often end with the word part -ly and they can describe a verb, an adjective, or another adverb.*

Extending the Lesson

Tape the sentence strips to the board. Have students identify each adverb, circle it, and underline the word each adverb describes.

On Your Own

Have students copy the sentences from the margin. Tell them to underline the adverbs and label whether they describe how, when, or where something happened.

You Will Need

- Writer's Handbook, page 27
- chart paper and marker
- sentence strips with the following sentences written on them:
  I ate slowly.
  She dressed nicely for the party.
  My mom jogged quickly.
  He came to school immediately.
- tape
- paper and pencil for each student

---

1. I ran <u>fast</u> on the way home. [how]

2. He threw the ball <u>hard</u>. [how]

3. Alicia bought new shoes <u>yesterday</u>. [when]

4. Danica came to my house <u>today</u>. [when]

5. Mom and Dad ate <u>slowly</u> at the restaurant. [how]

 Assess Progress

Note whether students are able to identify and use adverbs. Provide additional practice if necessary.

Theme 16

Review Adverbs

Lesson Background

An adverb tells *how, where,* or *when* something happens. Adverbs modify verbs, adjectives, or other adverbs.

Teaching the Lesson

- To review adverbs, read aloud the relevant portion of page 27 of the Writer's Handbook as students follow along.
- Remind students that adverbs are words that tell *how, where,* or *when* an action happens. They can also describe verbs, adjectives, or other adverbs.
- Tape the sentence strips to the board. Ask students to identify the adverb and the verb it describes in each sentence. Then ask students to determine whether the adverb tells how, when, or where. Remind students adverbs often end in *-ly.*
- Review the definition of an adverb with students. *An adverb is a word that tells how, where, or when an action happens. Adverbs can end with the word part -ly and describe verbs, adjectives, or other adverbs.*

Extending the Lesson

Show students a picture of athletes or dancers engaged in activity. Ask students to write on chart paper sentences that include an adverb about the picture. Circle each adverb. Classify the adverbs into three categories based on whether they describe how, where, or when.

On Your Own

Ask students to write three sentences describing a trip they took somewhere. Have students include at least one adverb per sentence. After the students have written their sentences, ask them to exchange papers with a partner and underline the adverbs.

You Will Need

- Writer's Handbook, page 27
- sentence strips with the following sentences written on them:
  Shannon will run tomorrow.
  Nadia ate soup yesterday.
  Papa put the newspaper here.
  The students were cheering loudly in the stands.
  She slept quietly.
  The mouse crept softly.
- tape
- chart paper and marker
- a picture of people engaged in an activity, such as a sport.
- paper and pencil for each student

Assess Progress

Note whether students are able to identify and use adverbs. Provide additional practice if necessary.

Name_____ Date_____

Story Organizer

Setting
_____

Characters
_____

_____

_____

Problem

Events

1. _____

2. _____

3. _____

Conclusion
_____

Name_____ Date_____

Sequence Organizer

┌─────────────────────────────┐   ┌─────────────────────────────┐
│ **Step 1**   │   │ **Step 2**   │
│   │   │   │
│   │   │   │
│   │   │   │
│   │ │   │
│   │   │   │
│_____│   │_____│
└─────────────────────────────┘   └─────────────────────────────┘

┌─────────────────────────────┐   ┌─────────────────────────────┐
│ **Step 3**   │   │ **Step 4**   │
│   │   │   │
│   │   │   │
│   │ │   │
│   │   │   │
│   │   │   │
│_____│   │_____│
└─────────────────────────────┘   └─────────────────────────────┘

┌─────────────────────────────┐
│ **Step 5**   │
│   │
│   │
│   │
│   │
│_____│
└─────────────────────────────┘

Name_____ Date_____

Problem and Solution Organizer

Characters	Setting

Problem

Events

Solution

Name _____ Date _____

Report Organizer

Topic Sentence

_____

Supporting Details

_____

_____

_____

Supporting Details

_____

_____

_____

Supporting Details

_____

_____

_____

Conclusion Sentence

_____

Name _____ Date _____

Poem Organizer

Image	Descriptive Words

Main Idea and Details Organizer

Detail

Main Idea

Detail

Detail

Name_____ Date_____

Cause and Effect Organizer

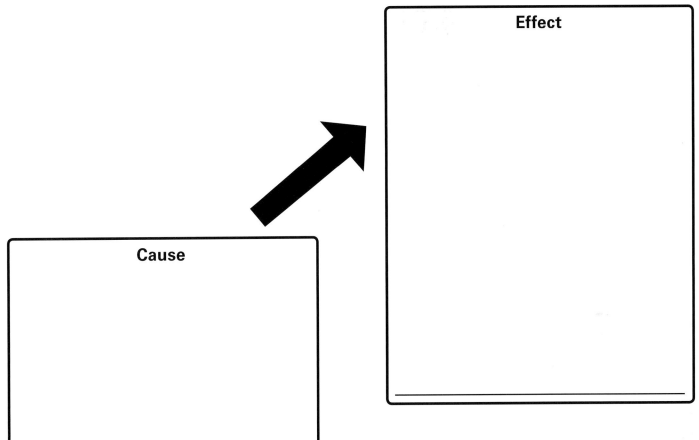

Effect

Cause

Effect

Name _____ Date _____

Observation Log Organizer

Date	What it looked like . . .	
What	_____	
	_____	
	_____	
	_____	

Date	What it looked like . . .	
What	_____	
	_____	
	_____	
	_____	

Date	What it looked like . . .	
What	_____	
	_____	
	_____	
	_____	

Name _____ Date _____

Sequence Organizer

Step 1		**Step 2**

Step 3		**Step 4**

Step 5		**Step 6**

Name _____ Date _____

Procedural Organizer

Process _____

Step 1

↓

Step 2

↓

Step 3

↓

Step 4

↓

Step 5

↓

Explain

Name _____ Date _____

Story Organizer

Setting

_____

Characters

_____

_____

_____

Problem

_____

Events

1. _____

_____

2. _____

_____

3. _____

_____

Conclusion

_____

Name_____ Date_____

Compare and Contrast Organizer

1.	2.
_____	_____
_____	_____
_____	_____

Compare and Contrast Organizer

Name_____ Date _____

Problem and Solution Organizer

Characters	Setting

Problem

Events

Solution

Name _____ Date _____

Personal Narrative Organizer

Main Idea

_____

Event 1	Feelings
	_____
	_____
	_____
_____	_____

Event 2	Feelings
	_____
	_____
	_____
_____	_____

Event 3	Feelings
	_____
	_____
	_____
_____	_____

Conclusion

_____

Personal Narrative Organizer

Name _____ Date _____

Main Idea and Details Organizer

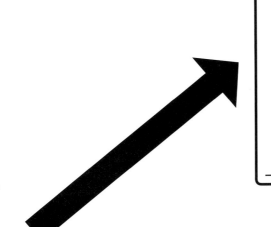

Detail

Main Idea

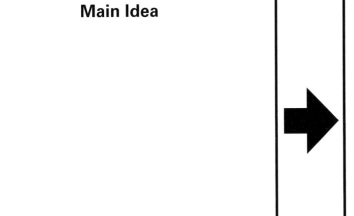

Detail

Detail

Name ______________________________ Date ______________

Letter Organizer

Date

Salutation

Body

Closing

Create an Atmosphere

Lesson Background

The setting of a story can help the reader "see" where and when the events take place. A writer can create the mood by describing a detailed setting. Students can begin to understand setting by describing the time and place. This lesson will focus on using the time and place of the selection to bring the setting to life.

Teaching the Lesson

- Copy and distribute the Establish Setting Master on page 50 of this guide. You may wish to make a transparency of this page for use during whole-class instruction.
- Read the selection "The Camping Trip" aloud as students follow along.
- After reading, discuss the selection with students. *Where does the story take place?* (a campsite) *Does the story's setting tell us when the story happened?* (no) *As a reader, could you picture the setting of the story?* (no)
- Tell students that a good setting tells the reader about the time and place in a story. Brainstorm with students some possible ways to incorporate details about the time of the year the selection took place. You may wish to ask *What is the weather like when Dean and his family go on the hike? Is it cold outside when they are sitting around the fire? What season is it?*
- Have students revise "The Camping Trip" to include details about the setting. They may record a class suggestion or write about a setting of their own.

Extending the Lesson

During small-group writing instruction, have students select from their writing folder a recent piece of writing that they feel needs a more established setting. Support students as they revise their writing. Then compare the original and revised versions as a group.

On Your Own

Have students look through other fiction and nonfiction texts in search of settings that engage the reader. Encourage students to record some of these examples of establishing setting in their Writer's Notebook.

Assess Progress

Note whether students are able to establish setting in their own writing. Provide additional practice if necessary.

The Camping Trip

Dean and his family went on a camping trip. They drove three hours to get to the campsite. Dean helped his brother put the tent together. Later that day, Dean and his family went for a hike. They were gone for a long time. When they got back to the campsite, they cooked dinner. Dean picked up a bunch of sticks to use for a fire. Then he helped build a big fire to cook the food. After they ate dinner, Dean and his family roasted marshmallows. Then they sat around the fire until it got dark.

Rewrite the Setting

Rewrite the "The Camping Trip" to include details about the time of the year the trip took place.

_____

_____

_____

_____

Make Your Ideas Clear

Lesson Background

Effective writing includes paragraphs that support a main idea. Supporting details provide the structure for a paragraph. This lesson focuses on building strong paragraphs by adding supporting details.

Teaching the Lesson

- Copy and distribute the Build Strong Paragraphs Master on page 52 of this guide. You may wish to make a transparency of this page for use during whole-class instruction.
- Read the selection "Take a Train Ride" aloud as students follow along.
- After reading, discuss the selection with students. *What details are included in the selection?* (*e.g.,* Train engines come in many different colors.) *Do all the details relate to the same idea?* (no) *What supporting details could be added to the paragraph?* (*e.g.,* the percentage of Americans who travel by train)
- Tell students that writers craft strong paragraphs to make a piece of writing interesting to the reader. One way to build strong paragraphs is to add supporting details about the topic. As a class, brainstorm ways to add supporting details to the selection.
- Have students edit "Take a Train Ride" by taking out details that don't support the main idea of the paragraph. They may record a class suggestion or edit the details on their own.

Extending the Lesson

During small-group writing instruction, have students select from their writing folder a recent piece of writing that they feel needs more supporting details. Support students as they revise their writing. Then compare the original and revised versions as a group.

On Your Own

Have students look through other fiction and nonfiction texts in search of strong paragraphs that engage the reader with supporting details. Encourage students to record some of these passages in their Writer's Notebook as examples of strong paragraphs with supporting details.

Assess Progress

Note whether students are able to craft strong paragraphs using supporting details. Provide additional practice if necessary.

Take a Train Ride

People have used trains as a form of transportation for a long time. Many people like to travel on trains. Steam engines were invented in England in the late 1700s. The Baltimore and Ohio Railroad was the first train company in North America. Train engines come in many different colors. Many U.S. presidents have used the railroads for traveling. Trains were the safest form of transportation many years ago. Today trains can go very fast.

Rewrite with Supporting Details

Cross out sentences that do not add support to the paragraph. Rewrite the new paragraph on the lines below.

_____

_____

_____

_____

_____

_____

Create a Unique Vision

Lesson Background

Effective writers find unique ways to express themselves. Many creative writers use figurative language to "show" instead of "tell." This lesson will focus on including metaphors in students' writing.

Teaching the Lesson

- Copy and distribute the Include Figurative Language Master on page 54 of this guide. You may wish to make a transparency of this page for use during whole-class instruction.

- Read both versions of the selection "Cool Cows" aloud as students follow along.

- After reading, discuss both versions with students. *How is the language in the first version of "Cool Cows" different from the second version?* (The first version doesn't use any interesting language.) *As a reader, which version do you like better?* (the second version) *Which version uses unique language?* (the second version)

- Explain to students that using figurative language helps paint a picture for the reader. A metaphor is an example of figurative language that writers use to describe an object or event. A metaphor compares two things that are not really alike, for example, *The sky was a sea of blue*, without using the words *like* or *as*. Have students find other examples of metaphors in the second version of "Cool Cows." Ask students to suggest other metaphors they might add to the first version of "Cool Cows." To get them started, you might ask *What are some ways you would describe a cow? What are some words you think of when you hear the word* cow?

- Have students write their own version of "Cool Cows." They may record a class suggestion or write a version of their own.

Extending the Lesson

During small-group writing instruction, have students select from their writing folder a recent piece of writing that they feel needs more metaphors. Support students as they revise their writing. Then compare the original and revised versions as a group.

On Your Own

Have students look through fiction and nonfiction texts in search of metaphors that engage the reader. Encourage students to record some of these examples in their Writer's Notebook as a source for metaphors.

Assess Progress

Note whether students understand how to include figurative language in their writing. Provide additional practice if necessary.

Cool Cows

Version 1

Cows are big animals that walk very slowly. They like to eat grass all the time. Some people think cows can sense when it is going to rain. They sit down when it rains.

Version 2

Cows are a farmer's lawnmower. They are hay-eating machines. They are snails as they walk through the fields. Cows are the gentle keepers of the valley. When it rains, they nestle in the grassy fields.

Use Figurative Language
Write your own version of "Cool Cows" using metaphors.

_____

_____

_____

_____

_____

Engage Your Reader with a Lively Beginning

Lesson Background

It is important to begin a piece of writing with a lively opening. Writers can use one of several techniques to create a strong introduction. Some writers begin by describing a scene in detail, while others present the big picture about a topic. This lesson will focus on using the big picture as part of an effective beginning.

Teaching the Lesson

- Copy and distribute the Start Strong Master on page 56 of this guide. You may wish to make a transparency of this page for use during whole-class instruction.
- Read the selection "Pizza Is Perfect" aloud as students follow along.
- After reading, discuss the selection with students. *Do you think any part of the passage needs improvement?* (the first sentence) *After reading the first sentence, were you excited to read the rest of the passage?* (no) *What is the big picture of this passage?* (People like pizza.)
- Tell students that a lively beginning helps engage readers from the start. One way to hook the reader in the opening is to give the big picture about a topic. Work with students to brainstorm possible ways to change the opening of "Pizza Is Perfect" in order to give the reader the big picture. You may ask *What information should be included in the opener? What would be a good way to make the opener interesting?*
- Have students revise "Pizza Is Perfect" to include an opener that presents the big picture of the passage. They may record a class suggestion or write a beginning of their own.

Extending the Lesson

During small-group writing instruction, have students select from their writing folder a recent piece of writing that they feel needs a more engaging beginning. Support students as they revise their writing. Then compare the original and revised versions as a group.

On Your Own

Have students look through other fiction and nonfiction texts in search of openers that engage the reader by presenting the big picture. Encourage students to record some of these examples in their Writer's Notebook as a source for strong beginnings.

 **Assess Progress**

Note whether students are able to craft engaging beginnings. Provide additional practice if necessary.

Pizza Is Perfect

I like pizza. It is hard to turn down the tasty blend of cheese, sauce, and chewy crust. Another great thing about having pizza is the large list of toppings you can choose from. You can add everything from vegetables to meat. Some people even add fruit to their pizza. You can order pizza from a restaurant, but it is also easy to make at home. It is not hard to see why many people like to eat pizza.

Write a New Opening

Write a new opening sentence for "Pizza Is Perfect" by giving the big picture about the topic.

_____

_____

_____

_____

Finish on a Strong Note

Lesson Background

A good writer ends a piece of writing effectively by using a strong statement or question. Asking a question at the end will keep the reader thinking about what you have written. This lesson focuses on using a question to leave the reader thinking about a piece of writing.

Teaching the Lesson

- Copy and distribute the End Effectively Master on page 58 of this guide. You may wish to make a transparency of this page for use during whole-class instruction.
- Read the selection "The Night Sky" aloud as students follow along.
- After reading, discuss the selection with students. *What is good about this piece of writing?* (It is descriptive.) *Was the ending strong or weak?* (weak) *How could the ending be better?* (It could be more interesting.)
- Tell students that a good ending will leave a lasting impression on the reader. Explain that one way to finish a piece of writing on a strong note is to end with a question. Ask students to think of questions they could ask the reader at the end of "The Night Sky." You might suggest *How many stars and planets can you see at night? Wouldn't it be interesting to travel into space?*
- Have students edit "The Night Sky" by writing a stronger ending. They may record a class suggestion or write a new, stronger ending of their own.

Extending the Lesson

During small-group writing instruction, have students select from their writing folders a recent piece of writing that they feel needs a more effective ending. Support students as they revise their writing. Then compare the original and revised versions as a group.

On Your Own

Have students look through other fiction and nonfiction texts in search of strong endings that engage the reader. Encourage students to record some of these examples in their Writer's Notebook as a source for effective endings.

 **Assess Progress**

Note whether students are able to craft strong endings in their writing. Provide additional practice if necessary.

The Night Sky

Have you ever looked up at the sky on a clear, dark night? There are small dots of light all over the night sky. Some of these dots are stars, and some are planets. If you look through a telescope, the stars and planets will appear bigger and closer. You might even see a shooting star if you look long enough. The night sky is mysterious and beautiful. There is still a lot to be learned about the stars and the planets.

Write a New Ending

Write a new ending for "The Night Sky" by asking a question.

_____

_____

_____

_____

_____

End Effectively Master

Try a Different Narrator

Lesson Background

Writers understand the importance of a distinct point of view in a story. A third-person narrator allows the writer to present the details of a story from the perspective of an outsider looking in. This lesson focuses on using the third-person narrator.

Teaching the Lesson

- Copy and distribute the Vary Point of View Master on page 60 of this guide. You may wish to make a transparency of this page for use during whole-class instruction.
- Read the selection "The Flat Tire" aloud as students follow along.
- After reading, discuss the selection with students. *How do you learn about the characters in the story?* (The narrator tells his or her own story.) *Does the narrator focus on what the character sees?* (yes) *Is the story fiction or nonfiction?* (fiction)
- Tell students that a story written from the third-person point of view is interesting to read because it allows you to see into the mind of more than one character. Ask students to explain how the story "The Flat Tire" would be different if it were written in the third-person point of view. You might ask the students *How can the point of view be changed? Who is telling the story in this selection?*
- Have students revise the "The Flat Tire" to tell the story from a third-person point of view. They may record a class suggestion or write their own using a third-person narrator.

Extending the Lesson

During small-group writing instruction, have students select from their writing folder a recent piece of writing that they feel could be written from a different point of view. Support students as they revise their writing. Then compare the original and revised versions as a group.

On Your Own

Have students look through other texts in search of a third-person narrator. Encourage students to record some of the examples they find in their Writer's Notebook as a source of point-of-view ideas for their own writing.

Assess Progress

Note whether students are able to craft a story using a third-person narrator. Provide additional practice if necessary.

The Flat Tire

I was driving to work early one morning when I heard a strange noise. I realized that my car had a flat tire. I got out and went to the trunk to get the toolbox. I was in a hurry to get to work! I was not happy. Luckily, a police officer pulled up next to me and offered to help fix the car.

Use a Different Narrator

Rewrite "The Flat Tire" using a third-person point of view.

_____

_____

_____

_____

_____

_____

Use Specific Words and Phrases

Lesson Background

Writers use active language to keep their writing interesting. By using specific nouns, a writer can name specifically who or what is in the passage. This lesson focuses on using specific nouns.

Teaching the Lesson

- Copy and distribute the Keep Language Fresh Master on page 62 of this guide. You may wish to make a transparency of this page for use during whole-class instruction.
- Read the selections "Life in the City" and "Life in New York City" aloud as students follow along.
- After reading, discuss the selections with students. *Which story interests you more?* ("Life in New York City") *Why?* (It uses interesting words.) *Are the nouns in either story specific and interesting?* (The nouns in the second story are interesting.)
- As a class, discuss why the second version of the story is more interesting than the first. Tell students that specific nouns can be a person's name or a specific place or thing. Ask students to list the proper nouns in "Life in New York City." You may ask *Which nouns make the selection interesting? What specific nouns could we add to make the writing stronger?*
- Have students circle the specific nouns in "Life in New York City" and add a sentence using another specific noun. They may record a class suggestion or write their own.

Extending the Lesson

During small-group writing instruction, have students select from their writing folder a recent piece of writing that they feel needs more specific nouns. Support students as they revise their writing. Then compare the original and revised versions as a group.

On Your Own

Have students look through other fiction and nonfiction texts in search of specific nouns that engage the reader. Encourage students to record some of these examples in their Writer's Notebook.

Assess Progress

Note whether students understand how to use specific nouns. Provide additional practice if necessary.

Life in the City

She lived in a big city. There were many tall buildings around her apartment building. She liked being in the center of everything. She and her friend loved to take walks through the park. She always brought her dog with her.

Life in New York City

Maya lived in New York City. Many skyscrapers surrounded her loft on Third Avenue. Maya enjoyed being close to her favorite restaurant, The Great Taco. She and her friend, Rose, loved to walk through Central Park. Maya always brought her dog, Polly, with her to the park.

Use Specific Nouns

Circle the specific nouns in "Life in New York City." Then add a sentence to the end of the paragraph. Make sure to use one new specific noun.

_____

_____

_____

Aim at the Right Target

Lesson Background

Writers should know their intended purpose and audience for every piece of writing. A letter written to a friend has a different tone and purpose than a letter written to a teacher. It is important to choose the appropriate topic and style for the audience. This lesson focuses on using a topic and style relevant to the intended audience.

Teaching the Lesson

- Copy and distribute the Adapt to Purpose and Audience Master on page 64 of this guide. You may wish to make a transparency of this page for use during whole-class instruction.
- Read the selection "Going to the Zoo" aloud as students follow along.
- After reading, discuss the selection with students. *What kind of writing is this selection?* (a letter) *Is the writer aware of who will read the letter?* (yes) *Why do you think the writer wrote this letter?* (to try to get the reader to agree) *Are there any parts of the letter that are inappropriate for the audience?* (Yes, some parts are too informal.) *Is the style appropriate for a letter to a teacher?* (no)
- Tell students that good writers understand that some topics and styles are not appropriate for certain audiences. As a class, brainstorm topics that are appropriate for a student's letter to a teacher. You might wish to ask *What topics are appropriate to include in a letter to a teacher? What topics are not appropriate? What style would be appropriate?*
- Have students rewrite the letter "Going to the Zoo" so it is appropriate for its purpose and audience. They may record a class suggestion or write a letter of their own.

Extending the Lesson

During small-group writing instruction, have students select from their writing folder a recent piece of writing that they feel needs to be adapted for a specific purpose or audience. Support students as they revise their writing. Then compare the original and revised versions as a group.

On Your Own

Have students look through other fiction and nonfiction texts in search of writing that is aimed at a specific audience. Encourage students to record some of these examples in their Writer's Notebook.

Assess Progress

Note whether students are able to adapt their writing for a specific purpose and audience. Provide additional practice if necessary.

Going to the Zoo

Dear Ms. Jackson,

   I think that our class should take a field trip to the zoo in April. It would be totally cool! We have all been working hard in school this year, and we need a break. Since we are studying different animals in science class, I think it would make sense for us to take a class trip to the zoo. I think we could skip the monkey cage, though. Monkeys stink! I hope you do the right thing and let us go to the zoo.

Your student,

Tamika

Revise the Letter

Revise Tamika's letter so that it is appropriate to send to her teacher.

_____

_____

_____

_____

_____

Name_____ Date _____

Editing Checklist

☐ My name is on my writing piece.

☐ My writing piece has a title.

☐ I read over my piece twice.

☐ I had a friend edit my piece.

☐ My piece is organized and understandable.

☐ All of the words are spelled correctly.

☐ I capitalized the first letter of each sentence.

☐ I capitalized all proper nouns, including people's names and the word *I*.

☐ Each sentence ends with a period, a question mark, or an exclamation point.

☐ I used quotation marks around sentences where someone is speaking.

☐ My handwriting is neat and clear.

☐ I used apostrophes to show possession.

☐ I checked my grammar.

☐ This is my best work.

Writer's Reflection Checklist

☐ Title of my writing piece: _____

☐ My favorite part of this piece and why:

_____

_____

☐ What I did to improve my piece was:

_____

_____

☐ What I'm proud of in my writing:

_____

_____

☐ Area I'd like to improve in my writing:

_____

_____

☐ One new idea I have learned about being a writer:

_____

Writing Traits Checklist

Ideas

☐ I have a clear message or story.

☐ I used important, interesting details to support my writing.

☐ My writing is focused.

Organization

☐ I have a strong beginning and ending.

☐ There is a title on my work.

☐ I put my ideas in an order that makes sense.

☐ I used words to show that my ideas are connected.

Voice

☐ My writing expresses my personality and feelings.

☐ While I was writing, I thought about my readers.

Word Choice

☐ I used strong verbs to show action.

☐ I used precise nouns.

☐ I used descriptive words that paint a picture for the reader.

☐ I used exact words.

Sentence Fluency

☐ My writing sounds good when read aloud.

☐ I used connecting words.

☐ I began sentences in different ways.

☐ I varied my sentence length.

Conventions

☐ I checked my spelling.

☐ I used capital letters correctly.

☐ I used punctuation marks correctly.

☐ I checked that the verbs in my sentences matched their subjects.

Presentation

☐ My writing is neat and clear.

☐ I used pictures, charts, or other visuals to add interest.

☐ I added a title.

Writer's Craft Checklist

☐ My beginning is effective and makes readers want to continue reading.

☐ My message is clear and aimed at my readers.

☐ I have included enough information and details.

☐ The reader can hear my "voice" in this piece.

☐ I varied my sentence structure.

☐ The sentences in my piece do not all begin with the same word.

☐ I organized my thoughts so my piece is easy to follow.

☐ My piece could easily be read aloud by another person.

☐ I edited my piece.

☐ I used exciting words that will interest my readers.

☐ My piece stays on the topic I started with.

☐ I wrote an effective ending.